Today's Divine Family

Living in Love, Not Fear

Robert and Deborah Hannaford

Blessings of Love

Deborah

Library and Archives Canada Cataloguing in Publication

Hannaford, Robert (Robert Warren), 1942-
    Today's divine family : living in love, not fear / Robert and Deborah Hannaford.

Issued also in electronic formats.
ISBN 978-0-9916820-0-3

    1. Course in Miracles. I. Hannaford, Deborah, 1951- II. Title.

BP605.C68H36 2012   299'.93
C2012-906407-6

Inner Search Centre

4 – 115 First Street, PMB 527

Collingwood, Ontario, Canada L9Y 4W3

www.innersearchcentre.com

Contents

Preface

WE ARE ONE presented their group consciousness to Deborah and me one fine summer day while we were vacationing in Wasaga Beach, Ontario. We were enjoying the warm breeze and observing the people playing on the shores of Georgian Bay. It had been a busy year, and we were enjoying some rest and quiet time at my brother's cottage. It was here, in the middle of the afternoon, that We Are One chose to reveal their energy consciousness to us. A great mass of energy with small, bright, flashing lights appeared before us; we recognized this as guide energy. I suggested to Deborah that she ask them what they wanted. She did, and to her amazement, a voice told her they wanted to speak to us later that evening at the cottage. We agreed. We were not sure what to expect, but we were excited and looked forward to meeting our new spirit friends.

We Are One explained that they are a group of 200,000 highly advanced spiritual beings from the ninth hierarchy, and their role is that of God's advisory council and earth's spiritual government. They relate the human experience to the spiritual realm. They required our assistance in spreading their message of love, peace, and joy to those who would listen. Since that summer day, Deborah became a trance channel for We Are One, which includes well-known spiritual beings such as Jesus, Kryon, and St. Germaine.

Why did We Are One choose Deborah and me? It is because we are physical members of their soul group. Also, both Deborah and I were members of Jesus' family over 2,000 years ago. Deborah was called Mariamne, and I was Jesus' brother James. We were close to Jesus and His teachings and members of that Divine Family; thus, *Today's Divine Family* became the title for this book. We have worked with the beings known as Jesus, Mary, and Joseph on many occasions in past lives. In this lifetime, Deborah has had visions and conversations with Jesus on many occasions. Through past-life regressions using hypnosis, her time as Mariamne and mine as Jesus' brother James provided insight into our roles in the Divine Family and Jesus' teachings.

We are also members of the Council of 144,000 Ascended Masters, as well as prophets, who are on the planet at this time. Our role, which is now in progress, is to assist the planet and its people to ascend into the fourth and fifth dimensions. We are here to teach compassion and speak about God's love for all his children.

One day, when We Are One was speaking to me through Deborah, Jesus came through and reminded me that I had a spiritual contract to write a book on *A Course in Miracles* (ACIM).

I proceeded to read the Course, and I studied it through Pathways of Light to become a qualified teacher. After several years of practicing and learning the Course principals, I proceeded to write a simplified version, along with my experiences. This is how *Today's Divine Family* came into being.

This book is to inform and inspire readers to purchase the book *A Course in Miracles*, to learn and implement its concepts, and complete the daily lessons. The ACIM book is required reading to prepare those who wish to ascend to a higher spiritual realm.

There are many who have already purchased the book and have read or partially read it, only to set it aside because they have found it too daunting. We hope to inspire these people to revisit the book and try again to complete it and work through the lessons.

Today's Divine Family is presented in an easy-to-read format for you, the reader, to have a clear understanding of the ACIM concepts. I point out the negative aspects of our personalities, such as the ego, and explain how to replace them with happy, loving, and peaceful personality traits. Should you feel uneasy while reading any part of the book, please note, these are parts of yourself that you may want to examine later, after you have finished the book.

For those of you who are not familiar with *A Course in Miracles*, it outlines Jesus' teachings of over 2,000 years ago to those who were spiritually mature. The text was scribed by Helen Schucman as dictated to her by an inner voice that identified itself as Jesus.

In addition to the concepts and principals of *A Course in Miracles*, Deborah and I include several chapters on other related spiritual topics, which I hope you find interesting.

Some of the concepts presented will be outside your usual perception of the world, and it may be a threat to your ego's perception of the world, as your ego does not want to weaken or lose its power over you. If you find yourself fearful at any time while reading this book, you need to know that this is your ego acting out its old programs and not your true self, which is the loving true essence of who you are. The ego is fearful of anything it does not understand, and particularly anything contrary to what it believes. I speak extensively about the ego and its role in your reality and your life script.

You may also find some of the concepts presented to be challenging to your belief system. You do not have to believe them; you just need to be familiar with them so that you may apply them if you wish.

Deborah and I are Divine Messengers for those who choose to listen and read what we have to say. What you do with this information is your choice.

Bob Hannaford

Chapter One
Creation

THE FOLLOWING STORY of creation was channeled by We Are One:

In the beginning, there was one great consciousness of loving thought, which is an Eternal Being you have named *God*. This is not a physical being like the one you believe yourself to be, but an eternal, omnipotent being unlike anything you can imagine. To look upon God is like looking at the swirling colors of a universe forming with its many planets, only without mass and matter.

God's vibration is total compassion and love. The love vibration is so great that it is beyond imagination, for if you took every loving soul on the planet and put them all together and magnified their love 1,000 times, it would not even be close to God's love.

Love is the only emotion within this magnificent being that relates to humanity.

As God was recreating Himself* to share His oneness, His consciousness divided into two beings. In this moment of separation, there was a momentary thought that you are separate from God, and with this thought was a question, "Does God know that I am no longer part of the whole?" The answer is that God knows that you can never be separate or not part of the whole, but the thought occurred, and in that moment, guilt was born. With that thought, a series of thoughts was created, which gave rise to the thoughts of today. It is important that you realize that the word *thought* is a special word. In the mind of God, a second or a minute appears to be an eternity in earth minutes. Let's pause for a moment and consider a dream or a daydream. You doze off for five minutes, but your mind, which never sleeps, creates a very detailed dream. You awaken and remember everything that happened, look at the clock, and see that only a few minutes have passed, even though it felt as though it should have taken

---

* We use the words *Himself* and *His*, although God is neither male nor female.

2

hours to create the span of the dream. All of what you record as history from that initial thought is just moments in God's dream. Although your dream seems to take place over a long period of time and appears complex, it is not when you are eternal.

Where do these thoughts of "I am separate" and "does God know?" which created guilt, take us? First, you created fear when you had the thought that God would find out that you were different. God is not concerned and knows you are not different and only dreaming you are. Your true essence is still the same. With this fear, a thought occurred that said, "I should hide this thought of being different." How do you do this when you are standing right beside God? You know that you are the same as God, but you believe there is something different. You decide to hide this by separating yourself and forming another that will then fix the problem of this perceived mistake. In order to hide, you created time and space and the planets and stars to create distance from God. This is a human thought, is it not? If something is broken, you get another, which will be whole. You

3

separate and separate until you create millions and millions of souls, all in the same likeness.

Second, after the planets were created, animals that were able to reproduce sexually were created. The souls felt they could hide among the animals, but soon they wanted to be like them. They created an androgynous life form that was similar in appearance to today's human form. The animals, seeing these androgynous forms, perceived them as good to eat. This was a problem, so to protect yourself, you created an ego. This engendered senses, which kept your body watchful and aware, and a primitive brain, which allowed you to flee from danger. The ego was designed to hold information and warn you of danger, like a computer program or security system. The ego was passed on from life-time to lifetime, telling you to be aware of this or that. In the beginning, the God self communicated with you and your higher self. After many incarnations, the ego's voice became louder and louder.

When the original androgynous beings of what is called *Lemuria*, the "lost land," met with the beings of Atlantis, they decided that since animals reproduce together, humans could as well, so the Lemurians decided to split their androgynous selves into male and female parts. Originally, the Lemurians' bodies were less dense than ours are today, and their descendants, the Atlanteans, had bodies that were less diaphanous than those of the Lemurians.

When these beings became male and female, soul mates and karma were created. And with the creation of soul mates, they found that their self-awareness and egos became so weighty that they could not agree on anything and were in conflict much of the time. When the Lemurians were androgynous, they could hear their higher minds and live through the higher mind's love, but when they separated into male and female, they could no longer hear their higher minds. They could no longer communicate telepathically, and they had to create language. Until then, all thoughts and feelings were easily heard one to another through the mind.

Third, with male-female separation, our thoughts became guarded and the ego mind interpreted others as a threat to the body. We created lies, along with fear of others, envy, and judgment. From that time to the present, we have had violence and wars and many affronts to the divinity of our true natures. The world consciousness is now at its lowest point and has removed itself as far from God as it can. The world consciousness has become so intense that people are becoming discontented. God has willed us to return to Him, and 2012 is the time of the turnaround. This is the start of the journey home. Over the next million years, you will start to take back your higher mind and give up the ways of the ego mind and see it for what it is. You are ascending, or traveling back in your mind, awakening to your true nature. We remind you of your Godly status and that you are God. You are still in Heaven; you have never left. You have only created an extensive puzzle that has now revealed itself, and you must shake yourself to awaken. The voice of Holy Spirit is the voice of God and has been with you for the entire journey. It speaks to you constantly, but you cannot hear it because you choose to listen to your ego voice, which appears to talk more and more loudly. This is a trick to keep you from ending the ego's existence. The ego is your creation, not God's, and it doesn't know or understand love. This makes it a poor guide in your spiritual journey home to God.

Fourth, you also created free will, and this is a part of your salvation because it allows you to choose between your two thought systems. How do you delete the ego programs and still its voice? There is a tool, just like the delete button on your computer. God has given us this tool called *Atonement* for undoing the ego through forgiveness. This is a way to let go of fearful thought patterns and allow for an awakening of higher thought. It allows a healing of the mind. It is your higher self engaging in a reality of which you have only a vague remembrance. God's love still resides within you. It is all you wish for. God's love is the universal healer.

Bob's Commentary

The message from Spirit provides a brief but good outline regarding man's journey on this planet to where we are today. Most people today seem to be wandering about in confusion, fear, and unhappiness, wondering where all the earth changes are leading. This is why God has given us a process called Atonement to heal ourselves by overcoming our egos and releasing all our pain, anger, and unhappiness. I speak about Atonement in chapter three.

Chapter Two
Separation

THE THOUGHT OF being separate from God, as described in the previous chapter, occurred a very long time ago and has been the cause of all our problems in the past and the present, and will continue to be a problem in the future. Every conceivable problem is a result of this simple event.

This event led to people's creating the ego (lower self) to replace God, from whom we believed we had separated. The ego, because it was not co-created with God and His love, was not created with love, with the result that it does not know what love is. Due to separation, all human relationships have become meaningless, in the sense that they are no longer based on unconditional love.

At the time of separation, we fell into a dream state in which we remain. We have been trapped in this dream of cause and effect for eons. We have locked ourselves into repeating patterns of pain and suffering.

Since humankind have been on this planet, there have always been advanced spiritual beings in the likeness of humans sent by God to remind us of who we are and to teach and guide us. The most significant person in the past 2,000 years was the man we know as Jesus, who is a world teacher. Much of what Jesus taught was misunderstood, in part because of our belief that we were separate from God. Jesus was credited with saying some things He never said. In many instances, he was misquoted, deliberately or not, to conform to what people preferred to believe at that time. The result of people's misguided thought process has been the basis for Western religion. Jesus came to teach us love—for ourselves and others. When you look around, it's hard to see what progress we have made in being His loving students or teaching His word. Jesus also reminded us of our divine inheritance and spiritual nature. We are each sons and daughters of God.

Humans, in our ignorance, have chosen to do things our way, which has resulted in all our personal, national, and global problems. Our schools and universities, of which we think so highly, use wrongful thinking in their teachings. This, in turn, has fostered misguided thinking in our personal lives, businesses, and government. All health- and crime-related issues are the result of that single errant thought from very long ago—that we are separate from God.

As everyone knows, business, whether small or big, is profit-oriented. While there is nothing wrong with being profitable, there is something wrong with our thinking when companies pursue unbelievable profits and aggressively compete to steal each other's customers in order to gain financially and in prestige. All businesses are always seeking new, innovative ways to increase profits, which, in the end, come out of the consumers' pockets. Most companies will say, "What's wrong with this? Everyone does it!" This way of thinking is a good example of the misguided thinking that goes on in our world. Few companies display a moral conscience, and those running them have forgotten or pushed aside their spiritual natures for materialism. Most no longer serve the common good or display compassion for the people they depend on for their existence.

Local, provincial, state, and federal governments are other examples of misguided thinking in the abuse of power. All levels seek out new ways to increase taxes and to mismanage revenues and resources. You have seen and heard all this before, but little changes. Those elected to serve the best interests of *all* the people should be expected to do so, and not serve just those who contributed to their election campaigns.

Most people in the Western world believe they have one life and have never considered that they have had numerous lifetimes and will have many more. While the concept of reincarnation is accepted in many Eastern countries, in the West it is accepted only by those individuals who are on a spiritual path. This knowledge is not taught outside of spiritual colleges and mystery schools in the Western world. It makes you wonder if people would be more aggressive in addressing environmental problems if they knew they would be returning many times until they learn how closely connected they are to the planet and everything living on it. It makes one wonder if we would behave differently if we knew that our every thought and action affected all the other people on the planet in perpetuity.

Chapter Three
God and Atonement

OUR CREATOR IS a loving and benevolent God, despite some common misperceptions that He is an angry, jealous, and judgmental being. God, in His love, created one soul in His image, which, when separated from Him, divided to become all the souls in existence, which are equal to one another. All souls were created as divine, loving beings who loved God and one another and lived in a state of oneness within the God consciousness. God gave all souls a mind (higher self), which contains all knowledge of God and creation.

When the souls separated from God, they created the ego to replace God. Over eons, we have forgotten our origin and our decision to separate from God and follow a new consciousness. Over time, we became more associated with our ego personalities. Everyone today believes they are

15

separate from God and one another, although this is not true. While we perceive we are separate from God and one another, we have never actually left the Kingdom of God. The only thing that has happened is that the ego conscious portion of our minds believes we have separated from God and no longer reside in Heaven.

After our perceived separation, God placed Holy Spirit in every soul's mind. Holy Spirit, inner wisdom, or higher self is the voice for God and is our direct link to God. It is a key to our awakening process, and a key to unlock the truth of who we truly are. As God has given each soul the means to return to Him, He has also willed each soul to return to Him. During our perceived separation from Him, we have subconsciously been searching for our way back to God. Because of our split minds, we have become more and more confused in our efforts to find our way back. Most of us have been consciously and subconsciously searching for God outside ourselves with no success. Some have found a way through meditating and mental searching

16

within their minds; however, more assistance is required to accelerate the process. Our ego minds become frightened when we speak of completing life on earth, as it fears death and cannot see nor understand a new existence in another dimension of reality in which it may not be included. If you are not ready to give up your pain, you need to ask yourself what is the benefit of continuing to hold onto it.

Since God has willed us to return to Him because He loves and misses us, He created Atonement to help us accelerate the process of healing our minds. Atonement means correction, or the undoing of errors. The errors are those misperceptions and beliefs that are not true, or are only partially true, that developed in our ego mind over many lifetimes. These misperceptions and untrue beliefs have to be corrected or healed before we, as humans, can move on to a higher level of consciousness and eventually return to God. Atonement is a call for truth, and by accepting Atonement, we have consciously preferred truth over illusions. God's truth is love. We embrace love when we allow Atonement in our lives. Atonement is available to everyone, and it is up to each individual to decide if they wish to develop spiritually at a quicker pace than that which their present path allows.

God has put Jesus in charge of Atonement, and everyone will have to accept Atonement sooner or later because God has established a future time by which everyone will have to be in the process. Jesus tells us that by accepting Atonement now, we will eliminate thousands of life-years of learning on the planet and will no longer have to suffer fear, guilt, pain, unhappiness, sickness, and death.

Atonement is another name for *enlightenment* or *salvation*. Enlightenment occurs when we discover who we truly are and realize many truths of which we are presently unaware. I elaborate on these truths in the following chapters. Everyone has to learn the truth eventually.

The Atonement process involves accepting the mind-healing (miracles) of Holy Spirit to purify the negative aspects of our ego thought system and eventually integrate it with the spiritual or higher mind. This means Holy Spirit will correct all negative aspects of our ego conscious, our subconscious thoughts, and our fearful beliefs; therefore, Holy Spirit will dispel all our fear, guilt, anger, pain, and unhappiness. We need only to ask for and allow this miraculous healing that is available to us. We have free will to choose healing over fear and anger.

Jesus tells us that any time we are concerned about or uncertain of anything, we can take it to Holy Spirit for healing assistance. We will be restoring ourselves to the great loving beings that we have always been. No longer will we have a limited ego thought system, conditioned and taught by previous generations, and we will join the more spiritually advanced beings of which there have been only a few from this planet in the past. As Jesus has stated, "Why would you not want to accept Atonement?" "Why would you choose to live with fear, anger, guilt, sickness, and death any longer than you have to?" No one can fail at Atonement as both Holy Spirit and Jesus will work closely with us, and at a pace best suited for us to ensure we do not falter. The Atonement process is designed to be painless and easy, especially with the divine assistance of Holy Spirit and Jesus.

When we accept Atonement, we will gradually release all our fear, guilt, pain, and unhappiness. We will develop self-love and a sense of inner peace and happiness. As we progress, we will learn what true love is and discover who we truly are, not the ego personalities our egos would have us believe.

Some of us will have a fear of salvation, as we fear love more than anything. Most people do not understand fear. Holy Spirit will reinterpret as truth everything in our ego minds that we perceive as fearful. The ego tells us life is all about fear, guilt, sickness, unhappiness, and death, with some happy moments sprinkled in here and there. All unhappiness, sickness, and death are due to separation and the ego consciousness. We have never lost God's love, which He sends us daily. We are not aware of God's love because the ego has created blockages in our minds.

Jesus says, "Most of you are miserable and believe this is happiness as you know no other way of being, because of separation." This is the way our egos keep us in a negative state of being. We tend to fear happiness because our egos tell us that we are unworthy, guilty, and sinful and, therefore, deserve punishment. If we look closely at our fears, we will see they are an illusion our ego minds created to keep God's love hidden from our consciousness. We all have difficulty in accepting God's love, and that of others, as we did not create love. However, we readily accept the opposite of love, which is fear—the symbol the ego stands for. Since we created our egos, they do not know and do not understand what true love is; nor do we.

Holy Spirit will teach everyone who accepts Atonement what true love is and how to extend it to others. This is easier than you realize, and we need to remember that God created us in love and we still have that loving essence in our higher-self minds. We have just blocked it from our conscious minds, and we require Holy Spirit to remove the blockages we created to restore us to the loving beings we have always been.

The *Course in Miracles* text is about love— the love with which God created us and which has been hidden by these blockages each of us has created. Holy Spirit's main lesson is to teach us how to love ourselves. There is nothing to fear as we have always been loving beings.

Bob's Commentary

When my wife, Deborah, and I mentally agreed to accept Atonement several years ago, we were a little apprehensive at times. We followed the lessons and were not sure what to expect. Having completed the Course, we can look back and honestly say it was easy to follow. Any time a new concept was introduced, causing us to feel a little anxious; we settled ourselves down and later wondered what we were fussing about. We know now that any fussing in our acceptance of mind-healing was our egos fighting back. You do not have to be a high school graduate to complete the Course, but you do need to have a little faith to carry through the process. There is absolutely nothing more important in this world that you can do for yourself. While there are numerous good self-help books on the market that you can spend your money on, no one can or will heal every conceivable problem you have other than *A Course in Miracles*. It addresses your root issue— the desire to be loved.

Deborah's Commentary

I have mentioned many times in our weekly ACIM group that I am now a happier, more peaceful person than I ever was before embracing the ACIM principles. It has helped me develop on a path that feels balanced and loving and helps me to stop the chaos before it starts. I cannot imagine being without it now as part of my daily life experience.

Chapter Four
Miracles

A MIRACLE, AS the name implies, is of a divine source. A miracle is a healing of the mind and body performed by Holy Spirit, which is an expression of God's love for us. The miracles performed by Holy Spirit are true miracles, as the healings that occur within you would not have happened otherwise. Everyone is entitled to miracles. Miracles have nothing to do with the laws of this world, but are God's laws.

When we bring a negative thought, belief, or concern to Holy Spirit for healing, the healing is instant in most cases. When a miracle occurs, our former problem quickly becomes a vague memory, and later we find we have little or no recollection of it; it's as if it had never existed. The problem had never really existed because it was part of our dream to begin with. Some healings may appear to take

25

longer; however, this is an illusion of time. While
we are in the Atonement process, Holy Spirit
protects our minds from further ego attacks. Fearful
thoughts may be given immediately to Holy Spirit
for healing when they occur.

The first lesson Holy Spirit teaches us is that
learning truth is simple. Everything the ego teaches
creates confusion in our minds, along with guilt,
fear, and unhappiness. Holy Spirit assists us in
removing the blockages we created in our minds to
gradually allow more awareness of God and who we
truly are. Holy Spirit searches our minds for those
subconscious thoughts that are not true and rejects
them, so eventually all our thoughts and beliefs are
based on truth. Holy Spirit perceives all problems as
being easily corrected, and all we have to do is bring
them to Him for Miracle Healing. However, we
cannot receive any healings unless we have accepted
Atonement.

- Miracles are expressions of God's love.
- Miracles are everyone's right.
- Miracles undo the past in the present.

- Miracles make minds one with God.
- Miracles represent freedom from fear.
- Miracles restore the mind to its fullness.
- No request for healing is refused by Holy Spirit.
- The Course tells us that God guarantees all healings.

It is necessary to bring all negative thoughts and concerns to Holy Spirit for healing. Should we decide not to bring certain thoughts or concerns to Holy Spirit, for whatever reason, we will hold onto them and remain unhealed. As miracle workers, we are taught by Holy Spirit how to extend love (forgiveness) to others, including those we may have thought impossible to forgive. When you extend love to others, you perform miracles for them as well as for yourself.

When we bring more and more negative thoughts and concerns to Holy Spirit for healing, we allow more light to enter our minds, and, consequently, we bring more love, peace, and happiness into our awareness. When we allow more light and love into our lives, we gradually realize we are all divine, loving beings, and we readily extend love to everyone. If we do not learn to extend love to everyone, we have not learned that everyone was created equal by God, who considers everyone Holy. By not extending love to everyone, we are being judgmental, thereby delaying our own miracles and salvation. In effect, we are being selective in whom we will send love to.

Chapter Five
Thoughts and Beliefs

I MENTIONED EARLIER that the ego side of our minds became a dream state in which we remain today. What we perceive before us is what our thoughts created. Note that we *perceive*, not *see*, what our thoughts create. All that we perceive before us is actually on a screen in our minds. Time and space are all part of the dream we created to reinforce our belief in separation. Space gives us the impression of a vast expanse between the planets and stars of our solar system. The vastness of space enforces our belief that we are separate from God. Contrary to what we believe, we do not actually see, and there is nothing outside of us. Everything we believe we see is a massive illusion in the ego of our minds.

There is only one thing that is real in our illusion, and that is love. Only the love we express for one another is real in our dreams. Absolutely nothing is real, including our bodies, of which many think so highly. Love is the only thing of a divine nature that we managed to bring into this illusionary world, and most of us find little love here.

The individual thoughts and beliefs we have about the world create the world we perceive in our minds. Beliefs are our thoughts concerning the nature of our reality. The big secret and the information that has been kept from us is that our thoughts create our experiences and our reality. All reality is created by our thoughts.

Our thoughts can be either empowering or disempowering. We are the result of our thoughts. To have a healthy life, we must believe in good health. If we have health issues, we can replace them with healthful thoughts. If our lives are full of peace and joy, it is of our creation. If our lives are not happy, and since it is our negative thoughts creating our lack of happiness, we can change through having positive thoughts.

We cannot blame others for what we experience in our lives. We are responsible for everything we experience, whether it is good or otherwise. There are consequences for every thought and word we have or say. A good or bad experience is the intent of our thoughts or spoken words. By being mindful of our negative thoughts, we can bring them to Holy Spirit for healing.

True knowledge comes from our spiritual minds and fosters truth through forgiveness. Perception, on the other hand, fosters a sense of being special and judgment of yourself and others.

- Your thoughts and beliefs are what you are.
- Reading this book will not change your misbeliefs; however, if you desire to change, you will learn how to do so gradually.

Bob's Commentary

I have had two events happen during the same week a few years ago. I was painting our bathroom and ran out of paint and had to open a fresh can. I had set the paint tray on the countertop. Having removed the lid from the fresh can, I carefully lifted the can into the pouring position. As I was going through the motions, I thought I needed to be extra careful to ensure I didn't spill any paint. In a split second, paint flew out of the can over the countertop and down the front of the cabinet onto the floor. I could not believe my eyes. Despite being careful to avoid an accident, I found I was in the middle of one. I spent the next hour cleaning up the mess. I noticed, though, that the paint had not spilled from the can, but rather, it had flown from the can as if an unseen force had been the cause.

The second incident occurred two days later. I had just washed a large crystal bowl and proceeded to dry it. As I was drying the bowl, I had the thought that I needed to be careful not to drop it. Before the thought had left my mind, the bowl was ripped from my firm hold and smashed to the floor. Again, an unseen force had ripped the bowl from my grasp. I knew I had not dropped the bowl.

When I looked back at these two incidents, I realized that both fell under the universal Law of

Attraction, which, in these instances, was that if you are afraid of something, you attract it to you. What you think is what you create. In both cases I was being careful to avoid an accident and unwittingly created what I didn't want. Usually you do not create this quickly, and I believe I was being shown how instantly our thoughts can create.

We have a friend who gets sick a week or two before going on vacation. He usually comes down with a cold or flu. Every time he tells us he is going on vacation, he says he will probably get sick just before. Sure enough, he gets sick. What he is doing is creating sickness with his belief that he gets sick before each vacation and reinforces his belief by saying he probably will. The moral of the story is to be careful of your thoughts, as you don't know what you could be creating.

Chapter Six
Perception versus Knowledge

PERCEPTION DID NOT exist before separation. The first split in our minds made the ego mind a perceiver rather than a creator. Before separation, we were co-creators with God, and what we created was real and not an illusion. We *perceive*, not *see*, what we create with our thoughts and beliefs. Time and space are all part of the dream to reinforce our belief in separation. Perception is a body function and is seen through the body's eyes.

Everything we see is an illusion, with the one exception—love. Only the love we express for one another is real in our dreams. Even our bodies are not real and are a projection from our minds. By thinking good thoughts, you create a good mind; poor thoughts create a weak and an unhappy mind.

Knowledge, on the other hand, is part of our divine or spiritual minds, which God gave us.

35

Through separation and eons, we have forgotten our knowledge. Not only have we forgotten, but also the blockages we placed in our minds prevent us from accessing our knowledge. Knowledge is part of our true being, which we all enjoyed before separation. Our knowledge knows who we truly are, and it knows of God and His kingdom.

- Knowledge fosters truth and forgiveness.
- Knowledge comes from our spiritual minds and never changes.
- Knowledge is power because it is truth, whereas perception is temporary.
- Perception fosters a sense of being special and causes one to be judgmental.

Chapter Seven
Forgiveness and Miracles

FORGIVENESS IS THE most powerful instrument of Atonement, which is very important to understand if we wish to awaken from the dream. Forgiveness is not required in Heaven and was created by God to assist those on planet earth with the Atonement process.

Forgiveness means learning to forgive ourselves and others for our negative thoughts pertaining to ourselves and others. I am speaking about those things we said in anger, or things we did in the past that left us feeling guilty or uneasy. Forgiveness is also used to forgive those whom we believe have said or done something hurtful to us. No one can hurt us with their words; it is only our egos that allow us to feel hurt.

Why do we need to forgive ourselves and others? The reason is that every time we have a

37

negative thought, or say or do something negative to another or ourselves, we unknowingly create guilt, fear, and anger. The more negative thoughts we have, the more guilt, fear, and anger we harbor within. The more negative thoughts we have, the more unhappiness we bring into our lives. I discuss more about guilt, fear, and unhappiness later on. When we sincerely forgive ourselves and another person, we create a healing miracle for ourselves and help the other person to awaken from the dream.

To properly forgive ourselves or someone else, we must learn to apply forgiveness sincerely from our hearts. There cannot be such a thing as partial forgiveness. Everyone with whom we have had an issue or grudge needs to be forgiven, regardless of what they may have said or done to us, even those you believe are not deserving of forgiveness. We cannot select those we wish to forgive and leave others; otherwise, we delay Atonement and remain feeling guilty, fearful, and unhappy.

Forgiveness, when applied properly, is

complete and unconditional. When we forgive properly, we find the feeling or sense of guilt or uneasiness lifts from us. To forgive someone and to still hold a grudge means you have not forgiven them unconditionally. True forgiveness is not complicated; we can feel the release of guilt that caused an imbalance between us and another. In some situations, it may be necessary to forgive someone several times before we feel a complete release.

Should we have difficulty in giving a person genuine forgiveness, it may be because we feel we are being asked to forgive a truly sinful event and overlook the truth. Forgiveness is not condoning a negative act. It is letting it go, along with the associated guilt, fear, and anger. When we fully understand that our lives are nothing but a dream, we should have no difficulty forgiving a dream event. Also, we were the ones who created the event that caused this uneasiness. I discuss this further in chapters twenty-one, on life scripts, and twenty-four, on karma. This earthly experience is nothing but a dream and never really happened. When we silently say, "I forgive you" to someone, we are saying, "I love you and acknowledge you as a divine and loving being, as am I."

With Holy Spirit's guidance, we learn true forgiveness and observe more peace and happiness entering our minds to replace the guilt, fear, and unhappiness we released. When we see the benefits of forgiveness, we look at all past situations and see where we carried a grudge.

Another area where forgiving ourselves is required is when unpleasant thoughts enter our minds. These negative thoughts come from our egos and should be quickly dismissed or cancelled by silently forgiving ourselves for having such thoughts. This prevents the creation of any additional guilt, fear, and unhappiness.

To embrace personal healing, you may find the following phrases beneficial. Use them often in your daily life.

- A past event where you were hurt and carry a grievance: Say, "I forgive myself for creating (briefly state the event and the name of the person involved), and I now bring this to Holy Spirit for healing."
- Someone has just said or done something to upset you: Silently say to the person, "I forgive you."
- Someone has said or done something to someone else: Silently say, "I forgive you." While in this situation, you are an observer; by saying, "I forgive you," you are not condoning what happened.

A common situation that calls for forgiveness is when we are driving and someone suddenly cuts us off, or brakes in front of us, almost

41

sending us through the windshield. Instead of cursing the driver of the other vehicle, say, "I forgive you" and go on your merry way. When we forgive the other driver, we notice a big difference in how we feel from how we would have felt had we responded to the incident in a negative manner, as we might have done previously. By forgiving the driver, we avoided any personal upset, which would have occurred had we verbally attacked them. Also, by forgiving, we left ourselves in a calm, peaceful state and didn't ruin the rest of the day by being upset.

There are many less obvious areas in our daily lives where forgiveness is required, such as when we are reading a newspaper or watching television and start criticizing those with whom we disagree, such as politicians, public figures, and sports figures, to name a few. It is not easy to choose peace over judging other people, and it initially takes a lot of practice to not judge others. God does not judge us, and by judging others we are placing ourselves above God. When you slip, and everyone slips now and then, quickly forgive the person you criticized and yourself and try to be more mindful in the future. By training ourselves to pay more attention to our thoughts, with the assistance of Holy Spirit, we become less judgmental and, eventually, non-judgmental. It is like learning anything new; sometimes it takes a little while to get it right.

Competition is another form of attack, whether it is one person competing with another or teams competing with one another. We compete with others because we feel lacking in some way, and our egos promote competition to make us feel better about ourselves should we win. Should we lose, we feel less about ourselves or that we are lacking in something. Whether we win or lose, we lose because competition is a form of attack against another, which creates further guilt, fear, and unhappiness. Remember, we were all created equal, and separation makes it appear as though we are unequal in many ways. Trying to prove we are better than someone else is to make ourselves feel better about ourselves.

We have all cheered a person or team to victory and enjoyed the excitement of the moment. In truth, we have participated in supporting an attack against another or a team, which fosters, guilt, fear, and unhappiness that can delay our Atonement. Many say they cannot live without their sports, politics, or other programs on television. I am not saying we should not watch sports or any other negative programs; however, until we can train our minds to be non-judgmental, we are going to be very busy forgiving ourselves and others. We have a lot more to gain by being non-judgmental, as this will bring more happiness, peace, and love into our lives. Competition is in conflict with our true natures and is another way we support our subconscious belief in separation. Recognize it for what it is and don't give it the importance that you may have done before.

Sometimes we find ourselves in situations where we are an observer and hear someone make a disparaging remark or an outright attack against another person, present or absent. This could occur when we are out and about, with friends, or at work. In this type of situation, the people doing the attacking do not understand what they are doing to themselves. To handle this situation, silently forgive the person who was attacking. Although this attack was not against you, by doing nothing, you are condoning the attack and creating guilt, fear, and unhappiness for yourself. By silently forgiving the person, you prevent any guilt, fear, and unhappiness for yourself and also help that person to awaken.

A form of attack we often see on television is where one advertiser attacks the competition, or where one politician attacks another. These are everyday examples of attack that we need to be mindful of and forgive those doing the attacking.

By training ourselves to be more aware, less judgmental, and forgiving, our demeanor becomes more balanced. We find our emotions become more balanced and we don't have big swings that leave us emotionally drained. When we become more adept at forgiving, we find fewer things upset us; thus, we have more harmony in our lives. We become more easygoing, less stressed, and more peaceful, which is what everyone is striving for, although few realize it. By being more peaceful and easygoing, we open within to become more aware of who we truly are.

In essence, when we learn to forgive others and ourselves, we acknowledge that they and we are divine beings, and we see their holiness and acknowledge our own. When we see others around us awakening, we awaken with them. Everyone is a divine being, and when we meet or see another, it is a Holy Encounter.

- To forgive one is divine.
- To love oneself is divine.

Bob's Commentary

When I started to practice forgiveness, I forgave those closest to me, such as my parents and other family members. I then looked at those from my past against whom I held a grudge. Later I moved on to forgiving everyone I could remember from when I was a child to the present day. Those whom I had forgotten were brought to my awareness so I could forgive them. Every now and then, to this day, a name from the past of someone who needs forgiveness pops into my awareness.

After practicing for several months, I began silently forgiving and blessing those I came in contact with when I was grocery shopping, at the dry cleaners, in restaurants, and other places, and I still do.

Deborah and I are both teachers of *A Course in Miracles* and have found some of our students have difficulty in forgiving those who had abused them as children or adults, which had created much pain for them. We encourage them to let the pain go and continue to work with Holy Spirit and the forgiveness process, and we have seen them improve within themselves. An area I have not fully addressed yet, and will do so later, is that we create every single event in our lives. When we fully understand the concept that this is a dream, and what happened in the past never really happened, it is a lot easier to forgive those whom we believe have hurt us.

Forgiving and blessing is a daily routine in or away from home for Deborah and me. It wasn't long after we started practicing forgiveness that we started to see results. It seemed that everyone we met was happy to see and talk to us. Our relationship with one another improved, and those family members with whom we each had minor issues are no longer a problem. Forgiveness really works.

I was an avid hockey and football fan for many years and played tournament bridge for over thirty years. By the time I had finished reading *A Course in Miracles*, I let go of bridge and I haven't played in over ten years, a game I thoroughly enjoyed for a good portion of my life. I no longer have the need to compete with others. With regards to being a sports fan, I no longer have the interest in my teams and suspect what remaining interest I have will gradually disappear. Since many of you who are avid sports fans or have competitive recreational interests will be reluctant to give up your enjoyable pastimes, I offer you this thought: Jesus tells us in *A Course in Miracles* that we do not have to give up anything when we accept Atonement, including any of our material things. We will, however, experience many changes in how we think about ourselves, others, and the world around us. Should we decide to give up our competitive activities, we will replace them with more inner peace and happiness. Eventually, everyone has to decide what is truly important. If we wish to remain guilty, fearful, angry, depressed, and unhappy, all of which fosters disease and death, then Atonement is not for us at this time. If we prefer to be loving, joyful, and peaceful, we will choose Atonement.

Chapter Eight
Ego

WHEN WE CHOSE to separate from God, we created a separate consciousness, which we call the *ego*. The ego side of our minds created a fearful dream, or illusory state, in which we have been trapped for thousands of years. The separation was initially intended to be a temporary journey; however, over time we forgot who we were and that the journey was temporary. The ego makes our belief in separation very real and fearful. The ego enjoys the power it holds over us.

With the splitting of our minds, the part where the Holy Spirit resides has almost been blocked off by the ego side, which makes it very difficult to hear Holy Spirit's voice. As a result, most of our thoughts and beliefs have become subconscious, and we would be very surprised to discover some of the beliefs that have been kept from our awareness. This has resulted in our being locked in chaos and confusion. The ego, if we allowed it, would control all aspects of our minds. Fortunately, most of us still have some connection to Holy Spirit, so we are not completely shut off from rational thinking. Approximately eighty-five percent of the time the average person is affected by their ego thought system, which influences all aspects of daily living from when we wake up in the morning to what television programs we watch.

The ego is that small voice in our minds that fills us with thoughts and idle chatter. It constantly reminds us of disturbing events from the past. Occasionally, some very disturbing subconscious thoughts rise to our awareness, and we wonder where they came from. We dwell on these painful memories and torture ourselves with these thoughts. We try to keep ourselves busy with various tasks that will take our minds away from the ego's mindless chatter.

The following are some facts about the ego and the illusory state:

- The ego is in complete opposition to God, and everything the ego believes and does can be considered anti-Christ.

- The ego does not want us to learn truth because the truth will weaken the ego's control over us.

- The ego does not know what it is and believes the body created it.

- The ego was not created with love and, therefore, does not know what love is.

- The ego believes that love is dangerous because it is unable to love.

- Every problem humankind has had is due to our choice to separate from God and to replace God with the ego.

- All relationships became meaningless upon separation as relationships were no longer based on unconditional love.

- The ego knows we spend a lot of time seeking love.

- The ego brought us sin, guilt, fear, unhappiness, pain, sickness, and death in opposition to life.

- Before separation, there was no such thing as death.

- The ego is not real and is part of the dream in which we are trapped.

- All power comes from God, and anything not created by God is not real and has no power.

- The only thing real on this planet is love.

- The ego seems to have power and control over us and at times can be frightening.

- All decisions made by the ego create guilt, fear, anger, pain, and unhappiness, and we do not realize how much guilt, fear, and unhappiness we have.

- The ego perceives everyone as being sinful and guilty, thereby making us fearful of others and appear as victims to everyone else. This fear enhances our illusion of being separate from everyone else.

- The ego always perceives with a negative view, which results in our feeling less or lacking, and therefore without self-esteem.

- The ego creates our negative thoughts, which, in turn, makes us feel unhappy. Have you ever stopped to think how negative your thoughts about yourself are? Probably not, as being negative seems to be our natural way of living, and people enjoy discussing their problems.
- Because we have two main thought systems, which are in conflict with each other, we get confusing thoughts about what we hear and perceive.

When we accept Atonement, Holy Spirit purifies all negative and disturbing ego thoughts. Once Holy Spirit begins working on healing our negative thoughts and beliefs, we notice peace and happiness entering our minds to replace our old misperceptions and thoughts.

The ego has little to offer us other than guilt, fear, anger, pain, unhappiness, depression, sickness, and, eventually, death. Holy Spirit, on the other hand, helps us remember the true, loving beings we are; the memory of God; and His love for us. We all have two choices: fear and death or love and life. Holy Spirit should be the favorite choice, for in choosing to listen to Holy Spirit we let go of the ego mind and embrace the loving healing powers of the God-mind. We embrace our true selves, our divine minds.

Remember that God has not forsaken us; it was we who chose to separate ourselves from Him, which was an attack against God. God does not see us as being separate from Him; we are only having a temporary dream. As soon as we decide to accept Atonement (the letting-go process), we begin our journey home.

Deborah's Commentary

As you read about the ego and learn of our misguided thought system, you may feel that this process of forgiveness sounds so hard to do. It isn't hard; it only requires a change in how you see the world and your role in it. Each day you bathe and eat. It is a repetitive function in the world. Each day, take a moment to welcome Holy Spirit to guide you and help you recognize what you choose to think and what you choose to get rid of. Each day you will feel yourself becoming lighter and freer from the heaviness of your old thought system. Be gentle with yourself. Don't fight your old ego thoughts, but simply allow them to drift off like balloons. If you forget to ask for Holy Spirit's assistance and you start to feel the chaos building, stop what you are doing and ask Holy Spirit for assistance.

Each morning before I get out of bed, I ask Holy Spirit to guide my day in love, peace, and joy. When I start to feel the chaos of the world taking over, it feels as if a motor has been turned on in my solar plexus, revving up and ready for takeoff. I recognize that my ego is trying to sweep me up in chaos, and I choose not to feel that way. I cannot see clients and write if I am out of balance. I immediately ask Holy Spirit to remove the misguided ego thoughts. I make a cup of tea and sit quietly and calm down. It doesn't take very long to become calm again.

Chapter Nine
Illusions

EVERYTHING WE PERCEIVE or experience is an illusion or dream in our minds because it was not created with God's love. Separation and the split in our spiritual minds resulted in the separated portion of the mind being illusionary. At this time, we may not understand or believe this happened. Everything we see is an illusion, even though it appears real because we can feel it, see it, smell it, and hear it. We created different senses to make our experiences real to us. These senses are an illusion as well. The homes we reside in, along with all the furnishings and the vehicles sitting in our driveways, are illusions. Everything we see is an illusion in our minds. They were not created in love, therefore they are not real.

To assist you in putting your illusions into perspective, I refer you to your night dreams, which

I call *dreams within dreams*. Even though most of your dreams are silly, they appear real. You can talk, see, feel, smell, and hear what others say. You know your night dreams are in your minds and not outside of yourself, and you know you will awaken from them.

In your dreams, you arrange everything. The people in your dreams are what you wish them to be and they do what you order them to do. Dreams show you that you have the power to make a world as you would have it. The world you make is clearly in your mind, and yet it seems to be outside. When you awaken, the dream is gone but you remember its details and how it made you feel; however, what you see in your daydreams is only another form of what you see in your night dreams.

We are trapped in our daydreams and cannot awaken from them, and this is why God gave us Atonement. Everyone's dreams, or reality, are different from everyone else's. The planet we see in our minds is similar for everyone. I say similar because everyone perceives the planet differently;

each of us subconsciously creates our illusions based on our own thoughts and beliefs about ourselves and the planet. There is a web of consciousness that describes the dream to us. We expect the sky to be blue and the grass to be green. What we see is what we believe realty is. We never know what anyone else really sees. Our beliefs about ourselves and the world today have been affected by events that occurred in other lifetimes, including our early childhoods. As children, how we perceived and interpreted events, and what our parents and teachers taught us, created what we believe about ourselves and the world today.

There are no outside events because everything we perceive is a picture we created in our minds. This may raise a question for many about why God doesn't help us out of all the problems we have created. There are two reasons: The first is that God has already created each of us as perfect divine beings, and although we reside in Heaven, we still have an illusionary dream in the ego side of our minds. The second is that we have free will to do whatever we please, even though our choosing separation was a poor choice. God could correct all our problems in a moment; however, this would negate our free will. Also, by interfering in our illusions, God would be acknowledging our dreams of separation, thereby making them real. God knows we are only dreaming and we will awaken when we are ready to do so.

- Only love is real.
- Everything else, including our bodies, is not real.

Chapter Ten
Guilt and Sin

BEFORE SEPARATION, THERE were no such things as guilt and sin. We created guilt to punish ourselves for our perceived sin of separating ourselves from God. Any time we feel guilty, it is a sign of an improper thought on our part. Our guilt, which we have accumulated throughout our lives, is a burden that we do not recognize as guilt in most cases. We tend to push our feelings of guilt aside rather than deal with them. Another aspect of guilt is that it is attractive to us; as silly as this may sound, it is true. However, guilt keeps many of us in unhappy relationships and repeatedly doing negative things.

The ego creates guilt within us, but guilt is the opposite of love, the true essence of which we were created. Because we have forgotten who we truly are, we associate with our egos, which we created to replace God. Guilt is used by the ego as a tool to lower our self-esteem. Everyone suffers in varying degrees from a lack of self-love. The ego has used guilt to keep us mindful of worrisome events of the past. These are the events where we have judged others and believe we could have done or said something different from what we said or did. Our egos are attracted to negative events that tie us to the past and keep us mindful of those things we could have done differently. The ego is like a huge database of old information stored to remind us of our shortcomings, pain, and suffering. Our memories can be very cruel indeed. This is the nature of the ego, whereas our higher selves would have forgiven and let go of these events, along with any associated pain, at the moment they occurred.

Closely associated with guilt are sin and fear, neither of which is real, although they appear to be real to us. Everyone subconsciously believes they have sinned in some form or another. The Christian religion would have us believe that we are born in original sin, which is nonsense. Much of our guilt and sin have been brought forward in our cellular memory from other lifetimes. Our Akashic records are recorded in our DNA. We all believe sin is punishable by death, which is reinforced by our religious organizations, causing us further fear and stress. We believe sin cannot be reconciled, and the fear of punishment by God causes depression, sickness, and, finally, death. Holy Spirit teaches that sin is not real and is nothing more than simple mistakes, regardless of their nature, that can be easily corrected, as outlined in chapter 7, "Forgiveness and Miracles." When God created us, we were perfect and sin-free. Contrary to what we believe and have been taught, we remain perfect and sinless. The spiritual side of our minds remains connected to God and does not know what guilt, fear, and sin are, as these were not created by God.

- Guilt and sin come from separation and ask for punishment, which is granted by death.
- The undoing of guilt and sin is an essential part of Holy Spirit's healing.

- In order to deceive you, the ego believes that sin is not error, but truth.
- Holy Spirit teaches self-love.
- The ego's thought system is based on the belief that our separation from God really happened and we are guilty for what we have done.
- Love and guilt cannot co-exist.
- The ego believes that sin is mightier than God.
- The ego creates guilt, whereas Holy Spirit dispels it.
- Holy Spirit does not punish sin but recognizes it as error and will correct it for you.
- The attraction of guilt produces the fear of love.
- Holy Spirit teaches you that there is no fear in love, for love is guilt-free.
- Sin is nothing but an illusion created by the ego. This is the ego's most holy concept.

- The ego, in its arrogance, believes it is more powerful than God.
- If you believe in sin, you believe in judgment and see sin in others.

The Course tells us that Jesus did not die to save everyone from sin. This is an ego concept created by humans, which many believe to be true.

I carried a great deal of guilt for over thirty years pertaining to a family situation that I thought was hopeless to resolve. Despite my good efforts and intentions at various times to resolve the matter, it seemed completely hopeless. My ego kept this problem front and center in my mind. I don't recall a single day I didn't think about the problem at least once. The problem was a major distraction and a concern, and I thought the problem may have been avoided had I said or done something differently years ago. My ego would not let me think otherwise. This is a good example of how the ego attacks us, causing more pain, guilt, and unhappiness in our lives.

I decided to study *A Course in Miracles* a few years ago so that I could become a teacher and course facilitator. One day I was doing a lesson that included a guided meditation, during which I was to take a problem to Holy Spirit for healing. I was a little anxious about doing this and wasn't sure just what to expect. Following the instructions, I asked Holy Spirit to heal my family problem. I instantly felt as if a tremendous burden had been released from my mind. This was my first miracle. Approximately ten days after my miracle and several others that followed, I sensed I was feeling guilty for no longer feeling guilty about the family problem. I was quick to realize that this had been my ego at work, making me feel guilty about not feeling guilty. Although this does not make any sense, it is typical ego nonsense that goes on in all our lives. I realized this was foolish, and, therefore, I was not going to have any part of it. I quickly asked Holy Spirit to heal me and was instantly released from the ego's game. Since receiving my first miracle, I have received healing for all my problems and concerns. If I sense something may be a problem, I immediately take it to Holy Spirit for healing.

Holy Spirit sees all sin or errors as misperceptions on our part, and these are easily corrected, with no scale of difficulty involved. All of the problems we have created are all related to our subconscious belief that we are separate from God. All problems and negative thoughts must be taken to Holy Spirit for healing; otherwise, you will not be fully healed and you delay Atonement.

At this time, Holy Spirit has healed every problem and concern I had. Any problems and concerns I am not aware of will also be healed by Holy Spirit. Being problem-free eliminates most of the silly ego thoughts that plague everyone's minds. When your mind is clear, it allows peace and happiness to reign instead of chaos, fear, and unhappiness.

We have a number of students who are in the process of taking the Course, many of them comment how their lives have changed and improved since taking this course during the past year, and how, by following simple instructions, they too have experienced miracles of mind-healing.

Chapter Eleven
Projection and Attack

THE CONCEPT OF projection will be new to most of you, and it is very important to have a basic understanding of it. We project our subconscious thoughts and beliefs about ourselves onto those around us from our minds. Another way of saying this is that those around us reflect, or mirror, our subconscious thoughts and beliefs about ourselves.

Everyone projects his or her subconscious thoughts and beliefs, whether they are positive or negative. What we project onto others, we judge, not realizing we are actually judging ourselves for those things we don't like about ourselves. We do not realize what we are doing.

Projection is the ego's main defense; it feeds the ego and keeps it going by continually creating guilt, fear, and unhappiness within us. This is the nature of the ego. If we perceive those around us as being unfriendly, unhappy, and fearful, then this is what our subconscious minds believe about ourselves. On the other hand, if those around us are happy and loving people, it is because this is what we are projecting. Remember, our minds create our own personal reality, and what we believe we are seeing plays out like a movie in our minds.

The above examples are extremes, and most people fall somewhere in between. Some days you meet happy, loving people and on other days people do not appear to be as friendly. In each situation we are seeing our subconscious thoughts about ourselves at that moment. How we perceive others on any given day or moment is how we subconsciously feel about ourselves.

There are many people who fall into the martyr or victim mode. If we feel everyone and the world about us are out to get us by abusing and taking advantage of us, we are victims of ourselves. Victims are not happy with life and feel unloved and depressed. When we believe we are victims, we attract negative events and people who enforce the belief that we are victims. If we are tired of being victims, we can change simply by thinking and stating positive thoughts about ourselves and others. While this may sound too easy, it is true. We can give that victim consciousness, which is a misperception of ourselves, to Holy Spirit for healing.

Everyone can change the way they perceive others and the world, if they choose. By changing our negative thoughts to positive ones, we gradually see major changes in ourselves for the better. We can measure our progress by observing the people around us and the people we meet in our daily routines because they mirror our thoughts. As Holy Spirit works with us and heals our negative thoughts, we find ourselves gradually becoming more loving toward ourselves and others. We also find an improvement in our self-esteem and our overall happiness and well-being.

A major component of projection is when we perceive/believe we are being attacked verbally.

Any time we believe we are being attacked, we become fearful and angry and respond accordingly. Any time we attack someone, we are actually attacking ourselves. The ego often attacks us by making us believe someone else is attacking us. When we attack someone, we are attempting to pass on our intolerable guilt to someone else. We do not consciously realize this is what is behind our attack against another. We cannot pass our guilt to another person.

There is an endless number of ways the ego attacks us, and here is a common example: There is someone you know, a family member, a neighbor, an acquaintance, or perhaps a co-worker who annoys you. One day you decide to give them a piece of your mind. We have all done this at one time or another and know someone who does it quite often. After the incident, you probably felt you were justified in straightening out this person. When you recall an incident of this nature, you remember you did not create any happiness and peace for yourself, although, at the time, you convinced yourself that what you did was warranted, and perhaps overdue. Although you received some satisfaction from sorting out this person, what actually happened was that you subconsciously perceived the other person was some kind of a threat to you and proceeded to attack them. While a verbal attack against another provided you with some measure of pleasure, you did not realize you had just created further guilt and fear for yourself.

Attacking another son or daughter of God is not God's way, nor is it our natural way of treating others. The whole senseless attack created by our egos brought us no happiness or peace, only further guilt, fear, and unhappiness.

Eventually we will learn, with Holy Spirit's guidance, not to attack anyone. Should someone verbally attack you, say nothing, but silently say, "I forgive you." This will prevent you from creating any guilt and fear. Attackers are, in fact, trying to project their emotional pain on us, and when we say, "I forgive you," we are declaring that we are not having any of it.

- Projection is the main defense of the ego for those who support separation.
- You perceive from your mind and project your perceptions outward.
- What you project on others is what you see.
- The strong do not attack because they see no need to.
- By attacking another, you are attacking yourself.
- When you think someone is unfair to you, it is because you requested that person to treat you that way.
- You have no enemy except yourself.
- The decision to judge someone is the cause of your lack of peace.
- When you are non-judgmental of others and yourself, you find tremendous peace and happiness.

Deborah and I work with ACIM groups of students. Following are a couple of examples of group members' experiences, where forgiving made their lives more meaningful.

Barbara perceived Janice, her mother-in-law, as being unfriendly and always attacking her on several fronts. This had been going on for many years, and Barbara dreaded family visits. When Barbara decided to accept Atonement and follow Holy Spirit's guidance, she decided to practice forgiveness on Janice. Every time Janice said something negative, Barbara smiled and said nothing and silently forgave her. This was not easy for Barbara, but she persevered, and it wasn't long before she noticed a change in Janice. Barbara realized it wasn't Janice who was changing; it was what she was projecting onto Janice. Eventually Barbara and Janice were able to have congenial conversations, and, occasionally now, Janice asks Barbara for advice.

Diane always had problems with her brother Rick since childhood. Rick always picked on her and created arguments, which was upsetting for Diane. Diane decided she would practice forgiveness on her brother every time she saw him. Over the course of a year and several family functions, it wasn't long before Diane noticed a change in her brother. Rick was no longer picking on her and arguments eventually ceased. Diane now enjoys family functions, although she feels she and Rick will never be close.

Chapter Twelve
Special Love Relationships

AT THE TIME of separation from God, all relationships became meaningless because they were no longer based on unconditional love. The *Course in Miracles* does not teach the meaning of love, for that is beyond what can be taught. The Atonement process aims at removing the blockages to our awareness of love's presence within us. We can't learn love because we have always known it, and it is located in our higher-self minds, which we have blocked from our awareness.

We are here to remember love, and through forgiveness we release ourselves from guilt, fear, and unhappiness. Through the forgiveness of ourselves and others, we understand God's love for us.

The ego's most ingenious device for deceiving us is the special love relationship (SLR).

The ego mind that attacks cannot love because it believes love is dangerous and it sets out to destroy it. If your mind does not understand what love is, you cannot be a loving person.

Everyone has had or sought a special love relationship. On a subconscious level, we are attempting to replace God's love, which we believe is missing, notwithstanding God sends us His love daily. We all believe we are attracted to others by their physical appearance, personality, intellect, kindness, the way they walk, and other reasons. We believe they will complete us and relieve our loneliness. In every SLR, we subconsciously believe we have sacrificed something to obtain love, and we hate the other because of it. You may argue this point; however, our egos keep these thoughts well hidden. As an example, you may have to give up some of your friends, things you like to do, and some of your freedom and do some things you don't like to do.

At one time or another, we have all fallen in love and enjoyed the euphoria love creates. It is as if we had no cares in the world. Our SLR runs smoothly in the beginning. While things appear to be running smoothly, the ego begins to undermine the relationship by drawing little negative, irritating things to each other's attention, such as leaving clothes on the floor, making a mess in the kitchen, and the list goes on. The ego is always quick to point out the negative aspects of our partners. These minor irritations, if unchecked, eventually lead to verbal criticism of the partner's habits, placing some tension in the relationship. As the relationship moves along, more serious issues start to surface, such as financial concerns, daily chores, personal health, children, and friends, which places further strain on the relationship. Before you know it, that euphoria of love you enjoyed has all but vanished and is complicated by arguing and bickering. Those who attack in an SLR don't see their partners as equals and retaliate to equalize the relationship. What began as a love relationship for many turns into a love-hate relationship, for which you can thank your ego. An SLR relationship is based on differences, where each partner thinks the other has what he or she hasn't. You come together to complete each other.

We also get confused between love and sex. Love has nothing to do with sex, and many confuse a sexual attraction as being love. Many use sex to attract love, which does not work. Everyone has a personal vibration, although many are unaware of it. The more loving you are, the higher your vibration is compared with someone who is less loving or who is confused about what love is. Love is of the intellect and the heart; it is of a higher vibration, which attracts others of a similar vibration and inspires love. Sexuality is part of our biology and chemical composition, which is of a lower vibration and attracts those who are interested in sexual encounters, and it is part of the ego world and its definition of love.

We have all had an SLR and were unaware our egos were systematically undermining the relationship by attacking us and our partners and creating more guilt, fear, and unhappiness in the relationship. Many relationships that started out as though they were made in heaven eventually erode into a living hell. Many of you remain in unhappy relationships because of guilt. God did not create anyone to be unhappy. The ego tricks us into believing all love relationships are built on guilt, fear, anger, and unhappiness. By doing this the ego distorts the true meaning of the love we enjoyed before separation.

When we enter a special love relationship, the relationship we perceive is far from reality. Many relationships have little chance from the beginning because one or both partners do not love themselves. If we do not love ourselves, we cannot possibly love someone else and create a lasting relationship. There are many who often change their partners as soon as difficulties arise and seek out another, only to begin the cycle of guilt, fear, and unhappiness all over.

The ego is the self-appointed mediator of all relationships. The body is the means that the ego uses to make an unholy relationship seem real. The body can be loved, but cannot love in return. Love of the body has made love meaningless.

When we accept Atonement, Holy Spirit proceeds to heal all relationships to make them Holy. All guilt, fear, and anger are removed from the relationship, so there is no need for either partner to attack the other. Holy Spirit teaches us that forgiveness purifies and heals a relationship. By learning and practicing true forgiveness, we can learn unconditional love. Holy Spirit teaches each partner unconditional love, which is God's changeless love that we had for one another before separation. Unconditional love does not have components of guilt, fear, anger, or attack, which are the components of the ego's form of a relationship.

Holy Spirit takes all the untrue beliefs we have regarding our relationships and purifies the destructible ego beliefs into thoughts of truth. Over time, a new holy, stronger relationship emerges in a gentle way that is not too disturbing for us and our partners.

When a relationship is healed, both partners are taught, not just the partner who accepted Atonement.

Some relationships may dissolve because the ego has destroyed them far beyond restoration; however, with Holy Spirit's healing, fully healed partners of a dissolved relationship can go on and establish new holy relationships. In a holy relationship, you see each other as equals and free of guilt, fear, and judgment. You no longer have the need to attack each other, which the former relationship thrived on. The new holy relationship flows more gently and is filled with peace and joy. Perfect love is in every one of us, and we need Holy Spirit to remove the blockages that have kept our love hidden.

Unfortunately, there will be some who will not have enough faith and be fearful of Holy Spirit and not accept Atonement. There will be those whose ego minds have convinced them that they prefer to be guilty, fearful, and unhappy and cannot accept love for them because they feel unworthy.

Who could be this insane and not choose Holy Spirit's gifts?

We do not know the true meaning of love; therefore, we are handicapped.

- The Atonement principle is love.
- Perfect love is the Atonement.
- The body was not made by love, yet it can be used in a loving manner.
- The love of the body has made love meaningless.
- We all have the power of love within us.
- We are all made of the same substance, which is the essence of love.
- You are here to learn to love, understand, and be patient with yourself.

Bob's Commentary

We have all been taught in the past that it is not good to love ourselves, for it would be vain and arrogant. We have created these silly ego words to say that one cannot be loved. Why would we create something that says you cannot love yourself?

We have all had a special love relationship that has failed or may be in the process of failing because of the ego's idea of a relationship. God never intended anyone to be unhappy and has, in fact, willed us to be happy. If you are unhappy, you can choose to become happy. The only reason you are unhappy is that your ego taught you that it is acceptable. Fortunately, we all have our teacher, Holy Spirit, within us, who is patiently waiting for us to accept Atonement.

Chapter Thirteen
Christ-Conscious Love

WE HAVE TWO main thought systems, which creates confusion about what true love is. The love we express for one another seems to be a mixed bag at best. It seems we love some people more than others, and some we don't seem to love at all. Even with those whom we say we love, we seem to attach different conditions to each of them.

Everyone has expressed love for someone. This form of love has a component of excitement because we are happy to be with that person. The love I am speaking about is reserved for those whom we perceive as being special to us. Although you love those special people, your love can fluctuate. You may have several children whom you love dearly; however, you may have one you love a little more than the others. You may have had many partners and friends over the years, yet one or two seemed more special than the others.

Unconditional love is the highest energy vibration on the planet, and it has been mainly forgotten. It has been deemed not culturally acceptable to love or to think or speak of love, although it is acceptable to speak of love in poetry, sonnets, and stories. This is most confusing to young people, who grow up not knowing what love is— how to feel it, how to think about it, or what the touch of love is like, and each generation becomes more confused.

To be a loving person sets you apart from those who have removed all emotion from their beings. Many have said love and emotions are weaknesses, which gives others the upper hand. Many consider displaying love is to show weakness. Many suppress love, believing it is not acceptable, even though we all seek it subconsciously. Exhibiting softness, compassion, and understanding toward others is considered not acceptable and a sign of weakness by many. This is a fallacy, as love gives you power, a far greater power than those who have suppressed it and put it away could have. It is our ego consciousness that tells us love makes us appear weak to others and that it is not acceptable. Jesus was a living example of unconditional love; it was His strength. We are all his students, trying to master our lessons in love.

Those who can see the spark of divinity, or God's loving energy in those around them, are healthier and have fewer problems with viruses and bacteria than those who do not see love in others. Those who express love know their thought processes are above the thought processes of those who cannot express love. They cannot be controlled and manipulated by others. They rise above, just as farm-fresh cream rises to the top of milk. They see truth in others and their statements. They understand people's conflicts between their ego minds and their higher-self minds.

The ones who love unconditionally are not interested in undermining others, but see and accept them as they are and are impervious to the control of others. Those who support the concept of power and control fear those who support love, for they cannot control them and are seen through by them.

Many of us have been taught very well to hide all manner of the feelings and emotions of who we truly are in order to obtain material things. Those who focus on love are getting ready to ascend to another spiritual realm and leave behind those who wish to continue with the old ways of power and control.

- Love is what created all existence.
- Unconditional love is a state of being in which God created everyone.
- Only love is strong because it is undivided.
- You cannot learn perfect love with a split mind.
- What is not loving must be an attack against others and self.
- The awareness of the body makes love seem limited, for the body limits love.
- There is only one energy and one true emotion, and that is love.

I was fortunate to have a very loving grandmother who always had a smile on her face for me. Although I didn't understand it at the time, I now know that she was expressing her unconditional love for me.

Chapter Fourteen
What Is a Body?

OUR BODIES ARE not real and were not made by God. Our bodies are a projection from our minds and are part of our dreams. Our egos use our bodies as devices to carry out their thoughts and feelings. By itself, the body is unable to do anything because it has no feelings or emotions and cannot see or hear. The sights and sounds the body perceives are part of the dream. The world we perceive does not exist, nor does space and time.

All feelings, such as pain and pleasure, which appear to be of the body, are made by the ego. The ego does a very good job of making it appear as if our bodies are real and tells us we are all guilty and sinful and deserving of punishment, of which the punishment is death. If we believe what the ego tells us, we eventually get sick and die. The body can no more die than it can feel. Dying is another part of the dream that we created to exit from this reality.

The body cannot heal itself because it cannot make itself sick; therefore, it requires no healing. The body's health depends entirely on how our minds perceive it and how the mind uses it. Our minds can heal our bodies; however, the body cannot heal the mind. We need Holy Spirit to heal our minds of all negative thoughts and feelings, which, in turn, allow the mind to heal the body. By accepting and completing Atonement, we no longer have to die.

The ego convinces us we will get sick and die. When the body appears to be sick and useless, we welcome death as our savior, not realizing we will simply create a new body and live all over again, a repeating cycle that has gone on forever.

- Separation produced the body.
- Your body is nothing but a projection from your mind.
- The body is part of your experience in the physical world.

- Using your body to attack is harmful to you.
- The body can act improperly when it responds to a negative thought.
- The body cannot die any more than it can feel.

Bob's Commentary

There is nothing outside of you that can be fearful or loving. There is nothing outside of you that can hurt you because everything you perceive is in your mind. God created all of us and gave us the power to create.

We have heard a couple of similar stories from clients, where their partners believed they would not live beyond a certain age. In both instances, their partners' fathers and grandfathers lived to thirty-five and fifty years, respectively; one partner proceeded to die on his thirty-fifth birthday, and the other on his fiftieth birthday. What happened here was that both men had this belief that they would die on a certain date. What your mind

97

believes is very powerful and, in these cases, each of these men created a heart attack and died.

I have two personal stories that reinforce the concept that the mind is more powerful than the body and controls the body. My first story began about twelve years ago, when I had this idea that if I increased my metabolism, I could take off about thirteen pounds, which I no longer wanted. I told my body, "As of this day, I want you to increase my metabolism rate by two percent until further notice." I had no idea whether this would work. The silly part of my story is that I promptly forgot the instructions I had given my body. A week later, I decided to weigh myself and found, to my surprise, that I had lost five pounds and couldn't understand why. Another week went by, and when I weighed myself, I had lost a further six pounds. I couldn't figure out what was happening. I wasn't feeling ill, and I hadn't changed my eating habits. It was during the end of the third week, when I found I had lost another five pounds and was now underweight, that I suddenly remembered the instructions I had given my body three weeks earlier. I promptly talked to my body, rescinding my earlier instructions and giving it new instructions. Eventually, after some experimentation with my instructions, I came up with the idea of telling my body to maintain my weight between 144 and 148 pounds at all times. Guess what? My body weight adjusted to the new instructions, and I haven't given it new instructions since. One thing I do each morning before I get up is, in the form of an affirmation, remind my body to maintain its weight as I had previously instructed. Many of you may think this is impossible; however, everyone has a body spirit that is responsible for body functions. This is to whom I gave the instructions. If you are going to try this, you must have a positive attitude that it will work for you. If you are skeptical, it will not work because your negative thought will cancel your positive thought.

My second experience that demonstrates the occurrence of mind over body happened a few years ago when Deborah and I spent two weeks in Cancun, Mexico. Within a day or two after arriving,

I caught a bug that kept me close to the washroom. In the meantime, we had purchased three day-long excursions, and I was concerned as to how I was going to manage them. I instructed my body to hold my stomach problem from 7:30 a.m. until we arrived back to our hotel room. Guess what? I did not have a problem during those twelve-hour excursions. When we arrived back to our hotel room, I headed for the washroom.

Chapter Fifteen
Last Judgment and Resurrection

THE TERM *LAST JUDGMENT* is very frightening because we believe it to be a harsh action taken by God against us for being sinful. This idea of judgment is a misunderstanding by people and has been handed down to us for thousands of years by various religious organizations, which, in turn, have fostered much fear and stress.

The last judgment is a healing, not a punishment, performed by each one of us with the assistance of Jesus. Everyone at some future point will look upon his own creations and choose to keep those that are good and discard the rest. This is the final part of the Atonement process.

One of the main reasons Jesus was here over 2,000 years ago was to set in motion the Atonement process given to him by God. The resurrection, not the crucifixion, established the Atonement process.

The resurrection was not a physical raising of the body, but rather a spiritual process of merging the ego mind with the spiritual mind, or our higher selves. In other words, Jesus completed the Atonement process while here on the planet over 2,000 years ago. There will be many over the next few years who will be resurrected like Jesus.

- Judgment is not an attribute of God.
- Everyone who chooses Atonement will eventually be resurrected.

Chapter Sixteen
Are You Special?

IF WE ARE used to comparing ourselves with our friends and neighbors, family members, and others in any manner, then we feel we are special. When we compare ourselves with others, we perceive ourselves as being special or better. This is something everyone does without realizing what they are actually doing and why. When we perceive weaknesses in others that we do not perceive in ourselves, we are substituting love for judgment by comparing ourselves with them. We judge others for not being like us. Some of the more common comparisons we make are about having more abundance than someone else, or having a newer or more expensive vehicle than our neighbor, or better clothes, home, or education, just to name a few. I am sure we can each make a list of our own.

If we are special, we have made enemies of

those individuals we have compared ourselves with, and whom we see as different from us. Being special fosters grounds for attack against those individuals whom we perceive as being beneath us or not as good as us. Comparing ourselves with others fosters loneliness, jealousy, and feelings of abandonment. We cannot be both loving and judgmental at the same time because we would be trying to merge two opposing thought systems, and this does not work. The Course calls this insanity.

By being special, we are subconsciously trying to make ourselves feel better while disliking ourselves at the same time. When we dislike ourselves or have low self- esteem, the subconscious negative thoughts we harbor are projected onto those around us. When we do this, we are unaware that our egos are creating further guilt, fear, and unhappiness in our lives, which, in turn, fosters pain and sickness.

Holy Spirit teaches us how to love ourselves as we never have before. When we learn to love ourselves more, we open the door to allow peace and joyfulness to enter and replace any negative ego thoughts we have been holding onto.

- It is impossible to perceive someone as less than yourself without subconsciously perceiving yourself as less than another.
- The ego encourages you to make yourself feel special.

Bob's Commentary

Whenever there are two or more people having a conversation, invariably comparison and judgment enters. When you find yourself in this situation and you are working with Holy Spirit, you need to silently forgive the person who is doing the comparing to avoid condoning their attack against another and avoid creating guilt, fear, and unhappiness for yourself. Take a moment and make a list of your thoughts on how you see yourself as special from your friends, family, and co-workers.

When I was a youngster, my grandfather taught me how to play canasta and cribbage. We would play cards for two or three hours at a time. I enjoyed playing cards and felt good about myself when I beat my grandfather. As I grew older, I learned other card games. When I was in my twenties, I learned how to play bridge, which I thought was the ultimate card game. I played often and would read many books on the game to improve my knowledge and skill. I began to play tournament bridge, which was more challenging, and I often traveled to other places to play bridge. Over the years, I acquired a number of trophies and eventually acquired a life master title. I thoroughly enjoyed playing the game, and I won more often than I lost and liked being better than most of the other players. This made me feel special and good about myself. I played bridge for over thirty years and eventually quit and discarded my trophies as I no longer needed to be competitive to make me feel good about myself. We have all found things we like to do to make us feel special and good about ourselves. When you understand the underlying reason why you do these things, you realize what you are actually doing and why you do them.

Chapter Seventeen
What Are Idols?

WE ALL HAVE idols, which come in many different
forms, and in this chapter I discuss some of the more
common ones and why we have them. When we
mention *idols*, we think of stone statues of ancient
Gods worshipped by people of ancient times, as in
Egypt, Rome, and Greece. This idol worship
continues today, but in forms we would never think
of. Although we don't recognize them as idols, they
are nonetheless, and we seek them to replace God
and to keep the truth within our spiritual minds from
being known. Idols make us feel better about
ourselves. Our entire list of lifestyle problems stem
from our subconscious belief that we are separate
from God and one another and we no longer reside
in Heaven, which is the reason we have idols to
replace God and the love we experienced in Heaven.

We are all subconsciously searching for God's love, and in order to replace it, we look outside of ourselves for substitutes. Sometimes it is in the form of a special love relationship. There are many other ways we seek love and happiness. We may use shopping, eating, or collecting to replace God. We do not realize that we create idols to replace the void in our lives, which is the loss of God's love.

Our biggest idol is the ego, which we created to replace God when we separated from Him. Those who are more closely associated with their egos are less happy, more depressed, and fearful, and they have more illnesses than those individuals who aren't.

We idolize our bodies in many ways by adorning them with tattoos, expensive jewelry, clothing, accessories, and cosmetics, along with cosmetic surgery and spa treatments to keep us looking younger—and to make us feel better about ourselves. By making ourselves glamorous and different, we draw attention to ourselves and support our subconscious beliefs in separation and being special. Our bodies and their presentation become our idols. We are worshipping our outer selves instead of honoring our God within.

Many of us like to have lots of friends and believe that being popular brings us more attention and love, which our egos believe is a form of abundance. The ego doesn't tell us that if you had every conceivable thing you desired, you would still feel lonely and lacking in some way. The ego encourages us to keep striving for more, which is one of many ways it has control over us.

Many of us have low self-esteem and look up to others whom we perceive to be happier, prettier, wealthier, and of better social status. We look up to movie and TV stars, sports figures, politicians, and religious leaders to take our minds off our endless problems. By associating ourselves with these idols, we are subconsciously riding on their coattails, or energy, in an effort to make us feel special and to bring more happiness into our lives.

One of the most common forms of idol

worship fostered by our egos is the acquisition of material things, such as expensive cars, homes, furnishings, and vacations, all of which are to make us feel better and more worthy. When our self-esteem falls off the map, so to speak, we head to the mall to give it a boost by purchasing a new shirt, dress, or shoes, and other accessories. Everyone can relate to purchases of this nature. Whether it is a new car or a pair of shoes, we feel an immediate rise in our self-esteem. That good feeling, as most of us know, does not last very long, and before we know it, we are headed back to the mall. The ego believes that having money or material possessions provides us with power and strength, and without them we feel we are lacking. Shopping for material things is an addiction, just as overeating, drugs, alcohol, gambling, and sex are. We all have seen the problems and how they affected us and our families and friends. When it comes to material things, we need to look at our intention in acquiring them.

If it is to raise our self-esteem and to make us happy, we are searching in the wrong places.

- Idols are used to replace God's love.
- Idols are used to raise your self-worth.
- Idols are substitutes for your true reality.
- Your ego fosters the acquisition of material things to take your mind away from thinking about God. The busier the ego, the less time you have to think about God and who you are, and why you are living this way.

Bob's Commentary

We have a relative who shops almost every day of the week and has been doing so for many years. This person is an addict and cannot stop because she says it makes her feel good.

One of our clients purchases gifts for family members and friends to receive their love. He also purchases gifts for other family members and friends in order to receive their love. His addiction has placed a great deal of financial stress on him and his relationship with his wife. His focus of conversation with his friends is about his shopping adventures.

111

His basement is filled with boxes of items purchased over many years of uncontrolled shopping. This is a sad situation in which many find themselves, not realizing what they are doing, or that they even have a problem.

We have a couple of friends who like to shop for bargains at flea markets and garage sales. Over the years, they too have accumulated many things that they have never used and that fill their basements and garages. This again is an example of how the ego fosters the acquisition of material things to keep us happy. These people are addicted to looking outside themselves for completion, when they could be looking within themselves for peace and divine love, which is ultimately what they are trying to buy.

Chapter Eighteen
Materialism

THE FOLLOWING IS a We Are One–channeled session. In this session, Jesus spoke through Deborah to a We Are One group on December 3, 2006, on the subject of materialism.

Blessings be with all of you on this glorious day. It is of the concept of materialism that I have come to speak to you today. Many of you have been misguided through the ages by a misrepresentation of what I said about material things when I said that "you are to put aside all material things and follow Me so you might have eternal life." My message was that in order to reach Heaven and total love, you must put aside the earthly things of greed, envy, anger, and fear. These are negative emotions that are part and parcel of your body's ego self. You cannot honor them and honor love as well.

The concept of being separate from everyone else is what keeps you in fear, is it not? As long as you are in fear, how can you feel love, which is its opposite? When a magnet sits on a piece of paper and you put graphite on the paper, you can see the magnet's aura. When you put the two sides together they push each other apart. It is fear that pushes you apart from others. It is love that comes from within you that attracts love from without. It is your love vibration through the Law of Attraction that draws love to you.

So many of you have become trapped in your concept of fear, anger, envy, and worry that someone else might get the new car before you. It is these silly things that come with the programming of this world that distance you from love. Many become so distanced from their love source that they do not know what love is. They confuse the concept of love with their biology and think it is sexuality that is the loving nature. I say to you that sexuality has nothing to do with love as it is only your biology speaking to you. Only love attracts love, which is an intellectual thing of the mind. Love is intellectual and spiritual. Love comes from the top of your being if you relate it to the chakra chart. It is your lower chakra that relates to your hormones, which is your sexual biology.

When this planet was created, it was with a great plan for that of the physical experience. You are a spiritual being having a physical experience, which most of you have forgotten. When you come to this planet, you take on the lessons of physical contact, fear, anger, and envy, and also of your sexuality. You take on many different lessons so you may experience them. It is like going to a clothing store and trying on many different pieces and saying, "I look good in this, but I don't look good in that." You try on fear, anger, and envy, and when you find you don't look good in them you throw them away. It takes you many, many lifetimes and many experiences for you to say, "I don't like that at all."

A concept that has been bandied about and misrepresented is the one that said, "Cast off your worldly goods and follow Me." Also, the statement, "It is easier for a camel to go through the eye of a needle than for a rich man to get to Heaven." This is utter nonsense, for it is not material wealth that one is taking to Heaven. What is this preoccupation with wealth? One who is preoccupied with cheating and forcing hard labor on others for modest remuneration is what the concept applies to. It is the concept and preoccupation with being separate from God and others that keeps you from Heaven.

There are many who will go to Heaven who have great wealth. They have not taken anything from anyone and only thought of how they might serve others, and in the process of service have drawn much abundance to themselves. They, too, are on a journey of doing God's work and serving many. It is the concept of nurturing, caring, and serving that motivates them on their journey.

The one who is fearful he might not have enough, and that others may get it first, keeps this

116

one at a low vibration, which prevents this one from experiencing love in their heart. These types cannot see only love in others and do not draw Holy Spirit to themselves. They work only from what they can take from others. They see each other as an opportunity for taking, as opposed to service and giving.

You should not feel guilty when you have abundance. You should celebrate it because you have freedom in seeking out new truths, adventures, and love. Your life is not meant to be that of sacrifice and suffering. Life is to be celebrating the beauty and the bliss that is about you. It is to be celebrating the remembering of who each of you is, and the rejoining to the one consciousness that you are. All of you are with the God source and the Christ consciousness. Blessings be with all of you on this glorious day.

Jesus clarified several things that were recorded in the Bible that were misstated and not fully understood by those who heard him speak. This has created a lot of confusion for many over the past 2,000 years, and we thank Him for the above clarification.

Chapter Nineteen
Peace and Its Obstacles

THE BIBLE TELLS us the Peace of God passeth all understanding. At the time this statement was recorded, very few people on the planet had experienced God's peace; therefore, the populace had no understanding of peace. Once you have experienced peace, you know there is nothing like it. We all enjoyed peace before separation. God sends His love and peace to us each day; however, the blockages we created prevent them from reaching our awareness.

- Peace is a gift from God to which everyone is entitled.
- Peace extends from deep inside of you.
- Peace is stable relaxation.
- Holy Spirit gives the gift of peace to everyone who desires peace.
- It is a lot easier to live in a state of peace

and harmony than in chaos and confusion.
- Holy Spirit will use you to extend peace to others. It will radiate from you to those around you.
- Peace is a state of oneness with all.
- Peace is a state of mind where love abides.
- Peace is a state of stillness in the mind without ego chatter.

Following are some obstacles to peace:

- Lack of desire for peace: In order to have peace, you must overcome any desire to prevent it from entering. You cannot extend peace to others unless you desire to keep it.

- Belief in the body: You must overcome the belief that your body is valuable or important for what it offers. Believing in your body is a belief in death. Only your mind can bring you peace and joy. The ego teaches you that the body's happiness is pleasure. Holy Spirit teaches you that only your mind can be happy.

120

- The attraction of death: What appears to be a fear of death is its attraction. It is the ego that created death, which is the enemy of life. This is a heavily guarded secret of your ego.
- The last obstacle is releasing or getting over the fear of God: Everyone who has accepted Atonement has been brought to this point with both Jesus' and Holy Spirit's assistance.

Bob's Commentary

Initially, peace seems to sneak into your awareness in small amounts. If you have never experienced peace, you will instantly recognize it when it does appear, as it is nothing like anything you have previously experienced. Deborah and I have enjoyed peace for some time now and savor it. Peace is a state of mind that does not allow any silly ego chatter and upset to occur. Nothing will seem to bother you no matter how disturbing it may be to others. Peace provides you with clarity of thought and a state of well-being. Your mind is protected by

Holy Spirit from any negative ego thoughts that would have created confusion, guilt, and unhappiness. We are very aware of our peace, which provides us with increasing comfort and awareness of who we truly are.

Peace and unconditional love are the ultimate experiences to which everyone is entitled. You do not have to be doing something all the time to make yourself busy or happy because the components of peace are self-love, love of God, and love of all others. There is no substitute for peace and harmony.

Deborah's Commentary

When chaos of the ego mind likes to occasionally test us, as it will from time to time, I feel its presence like a buzzing over my solar plexus and heart centers. This is the ego's way of trying to convince me that the body is more than the mind. I clear this thought very quickly, as it is not my choice to be in chaos. I wish only for peaceful thoughts and a peaceful lifestyle.

Chapter Twenty
What Is a Soul?

GOD CREATED EACH of us as a soul, which is our true identity and is indestructible. Despite our subconscious belief that we have separated from God and no longer live in Heaven, our souls have never left Heaven and know the truth of our existence. Our physical bodies are connected to our souls by silver and gold cords that are witnessed on the ethereal plane.

When we first believed we were separate from God, our spiritual minds separated in two and we created an ego mind to replace God on earth. When this separation occurred, the ego side of our minds fell into a dream state, in which we remain today. The soul is not the ego; therefore, do not confuse yourself by believing it is.

Our personalities have been created by our souls, which construct our daily reality based on our individual thoughts and beliefs. The world we see has been created by our souls. Remember, the reality we experience is but a dream—a truth everyone will eventually learn.

The soul is always in a state of learning new things and developing as it learns. It is not bound by the limitations or boundaries that we have created for ourselves on this planet.

Our bodies are a manifestation of what we individually are in this earthly reality. In other realities, we have other forms. Yes, we all visit in other realities as well as during our sleep states. The journey of the soul is complex and mind boggling; however, some day we will all understand.

Chapter Twenty-One
Life Scripts

IF YOU HAVE lived on this planet, you, along with your spiritual guide and angels, prepared a life script for each of your earthly lives before your initial incarnation. You can choose any number of lifetimes you wish from several to a hundred or more. Your scripts are prepared in great detail, including the parents you choose and your siblings, friends, gender, sexual partners, intelligence quotient, learning disabilities, occupations, aptitudes, race, and country. You also choose your body shape, size, and health. Everything is prepared based on your choices before you are born into a body.

Earth is a fear-based planet, and fear is one of the reasons we come here, so that we may learn about fear, be controlled by it, and overcome it, eventually learning that it is not real. What is important to learn from our life lessons is whether we respond with fear, anger, and judgment, or if we choose to respond with love, peace, and innocence. It is like a survival test we create for ourselves. We also create the events in which our lessons will be learned. The concept of fear is introduced at a very young age by our parents in order to protect us from harm. What is used as a tool of protection can become a barrier to other learning.

Your life script always includes one major life lesson, along with many minor lessons. My major life lesson is patience. Also included in your life script is negative karma from earlier lifetimes, which you will work to release. I discuss karma in chapter twenty-four. A life script usually, but not always, includes forms of abuse you may wish to experience. You may ask why you would want to have an unpleasant experience. The answer is that how you respond to a negative event and overcome any trauma can be a great learning experience for numerous reasons that are not apparent during your lifetime.

Part of everyone's life script is death. Death

is the exit from each lifetime and usually is scheduled after you have completed your lessons. You don't get to complete all your lessons in every instance; some are carried over to your next life. In fact, many options on the script are left incomplete and not recognized.

There is a little flexibility in your script in some areas, such as if you have an interest in a person who was not part of your script. Since this person was not part of your script, nor you part of theirs, the relationship would be of short duration and you would return to your script. This person may then enter your soul group in future lives. The type of job in your script does not necessarily need to be adhered to. What happens in this situation is that your script is partially rewritten to include the lessons you chose to learn had you chosen one of the occupations you included in your script.

Your personality is part of your free will and is a combination of soul/your true self and your ego, and it develops during your lifetime.

Another area of life scripts are accidents.

There are no such things as accidents because they are part of your script and are events by which many of us choose to exit the planet. You may ask why you would choose a vehicle accident in which you are killed. When you are preparing your life script, it is your true self, or higher self, who is preparing the script, and it knows that life is eternal and your script is a dream. Some people choose to leave the planet early because their lessons have been completed. We often hear of a young married man with a wife and two small children who is killed in an accident. This was part of his script and that of his wife's, who has to raise the children without a father. In many cases, the teacher leaves through death so the student may learn. We are all teachers and students in our life scripts.

I have left the topic of disease until last as I need to spend more time on this subject. A whole book could be written on disease as it pertains to your life script. It is not mandatory to have a disease of any kind in your script. Some people have a specific disease written in for numerous reasons.

Some people have a disease to overcome, so they may experience the healing process. Some choose to have a disease so that people of service may help them, whether it is a doctor, naturopath, X-ray technician, or herbalist. Others choose to die from a disease and make it part of their exit strategy. Everyone carries every disease gene, and some have a predisposition to certain diseases. It is up to you during your life to activate or not activate any disease you have a predisposition to. If you have or anyone in your family has a predisposition to cancer, for example, it does not mean you will get cancer unless you choose to experience it. Remember, you are not a victim of your body. This is an ego concept. The truth is that you are in control of your body, and if you don't wish to be sick, tell your body.

Many people relish their illnesses because illness gives them something to talk about to those who will listen, plus it draws attention to them. It makes them feel special. Some choose to fight their disease, which makes it worse than if they had not.

Doing battle, waging war, creates a stronger bond with the disease. The Law of Attraction pulls the disease into their reality, not realizing they don't want it. Some people get cancer and believe it to be a death sentence and that they cannot beat it. Many create a disease specifically so that they can walk away from this life. Some people have a very short life due to an unfinished lesson or two from a former life. Even a baby or a young person will exit early from their life for a multitude of reasons. Who is the teacher and who is the student in every situation? Many lessons can be taught by a person's life choices. There are many things on this planet that do not make any sense; however, that was how this reality was created, to experience many things.

Bob's Commentary

You often hear stories of frustrated parents who push their children into college or university, only to have them drop out. Some parents push their children into professions only to have them leave that profession and choose another altogether different one. In some instances, children will seek out a lesser job, such as retail or a service position with a lower pay scale, which they have scripted for reasons known only to their higher selves.

Parents are often critical of their children's choice of partners and lifestyle and often get into abusive relationships with their children. Many people become drug users and prostitutes, which are outside their parent's scope of understanding. I have a friend whose son was raised in a loving and abundant lifestyle. This son chose to reject the opportunities he was given and live on welfare and have his two children placed in foster homes.

In every one of the above situations, the child is living the life script he or she prepared for this lifetime in order to learn certain life lessons. When you understand that everyone, including you, is living their life script, there is no reason to be upset and frustrated with yourself and others, as everyone is living the life script and learning the lessons they chose. It is their free will to do what they do, not ours to judge them. That is not to say that you cannot help another. It is to say that you should provide service where you can, but you cannot change someone's script when it isn't meant to be changed by you. You don't always know what is best for another, and age doesn't always make you the teacher. Many times children are the greatest teachers for their parents.

Chapter Twenty-Two
Meditation

ATONEMENT IS THE most important thing in the world you can do for yourself. The next best thing is meditation. We are all, on a subconscious level, searching for God and His love. You will not find God outside yourself, and only through meditation will you find proof of God. For thousands of years, people who have been seeking peace have been meditating.

Most of us are restless and need various activities, which give us a false sense of comfort. Activities create senseless talk, concerns, and stress, and often include acquiring material things to bring some sense of happiness. Our desire for material things results in our forgetting God and brings less happiness and peace into our lives. Most of us, when we get up in the morning, have no thought about God and how to bring peace and harmony into our lives.

The following are the main benefits of meditating regularly:

- It eliminates stress and improves your overall well-being.
- Divine wisdom can be acquired, along with other gifts of God.
- Peace is the first gift of God in response to meditation.
- You discover the presence of God.
- Through meditation you have the potential to become Christ-like.
- Focusing on God during meditation is the portal through which to contact God.

Bob's Commentary

I have found that most people are familiar with the word *meditation*; however, they do not understand what it is about. Most say they do not have time for meditation, and these same people are those who have little peace and harmony in their lives. Others may complain that they can't stop their minds' thoughts. Don't fight the thoughts. Try to let them pass.

Meditation is not difficult and can be easily learned if you choose to do something that is beneficial for yourself. There are many good books and CDs to teach you the most common techniques, and these can be acquired from most major bookstores. Meditation classes are offered in most communities, and you can choose from many techniques. Those who meditate regularly will tell you how much they enjoy it, and how it has improved the quality of their lives. If you wish to find peace and happiness, you will find it within your mind and not outside yourself through various ego activities.

I meditate two to three hours every day and cannot begin my day without meditating first thing each morning. Meditating seems to establish my peace and harmony each day. Most of you do not have time to meditate two to three hours. However, most of you can for ten to fifteen minutes each day.

A simple meditation is to close your eyes and silently count your breathing cycle. Breathe in and out and count to three, four, or five with each breath. Hold the breath to the count of three, four, or five and exhale through your mouth to the count of three, four, or five. Repeat the sequence and feel yourself drift into a peaceful reality without any additional thoughts than your simple counting. Do this for five or ten minutes, or longer if you wish.

Chapter Twenty-Three
Blessings

THE TERM *BLESSINGS* is generally thought to be associated with some religious rite and is not fully understood. Everyone has the power to use blessings in their daily routine. This is a God-given gift everyone has to improve their quality of life. This beautiful divine word carries more power than you realize.

When you meet someone on the street or at a function, by silently or verbally blessing them, you acknowledge them as a Son of God. Everyone is a Son of God and you are recognizing their divinity as well as your own.

You should bless your bath water and the water you drink. Even though we are told our drinking water is pure, it still contains impurities and negative energies.

Blessing your food before you eat it will bring wholeness to it and remove any impurities. We Are One tell us that "most foods, as you are aware, have been genetically altered, even though, in many cases, we have been told they haven't." By blessing the food and water, you adjust the vibration to one that is more agreeable to your system.

Bob's Commentary

Deborah and I bless our food, water, and beverages without fail. Blessing is a simple, healthy addition to add to your daily routine. Initially, you may forget at times; however, once it becomes a habit, you will do it automatically and feel better for it. You may ask your angels to bless your food, or ask Holy Spirit for a blessing. Simply say, "Holy Spirit, please bless this food vibrationally and nutritionally for my body and mind's higher good and physical needs."

Chapter Twenty-Four
Karma

KARMA IS A universal law of cause and effect where karma created in former lifetimes is brought forward into subsequent lifetimes to be repaid or undone. Positive or negative karma is based on your positive and negative thoughts and actions toward yourself and others. Good karma created from your kindness toward yourself and others will bring you abundance in the form of good friends, partners, and health, to name a few. Some karma can be physical in nature, such as a birthmark, stuttering, or a deformity.

Negative karma is about letting go of judgment of yourself and others through forgiveness. Choosing not to forgive may result in a disease and other forms of personal discomfort. I was given an example by We Are One when a person who had been murdered in many former lifetimes chose a script where he came back as a serial killer and balanced, or undid, his karma by repaying the debt to those who murdered him. In murdering those who had murdered him, he repaid/released the negative karma they each had created with him.

Everyone creates karma, and no deed, good or negative, can be avoided. A criminal who stole from others and who avoided prison cannot avoid the negative karma he created. In a later lifetime, he will have a life script where he will have to repay the money he stole. He is energetically indebted to the person he took something from. If a criminal goes to prison for his crimes, he still has his karma to deal with.

There is no such thing as an accident, only events that are part of one's life script. Anyone who is injured or murdered has it in their script in order to learn a life lesson or repay their negative karma. You often hear news reports where many are killed in a vehicle accident, or a busload of people are killed when the bus falls into a ravine. These accidents are all script-related. Anyone surviving the accident was meant to survive. When you have a fuller understanding of the truths outlined within this book, you will develop a different perspective of what is really happening around you and on this planet. Taking responsibility for one's life script helps you to balance your life events and, therefore, release yourself from the karmic cycle of birth, death, and rebirth. Many people keep reliving the same events in different locations at different times simply because they will not let go of the connection or take responsibility.

We Are One told me that my friend John, in a former lifetime, had shot me in the back when I was a town sheriff. He was helping me undo my negative karma with him, which I had created in an earlier lifetime when I killed him in battle. In this lifetime, John and I are friends who are interested in spirituality and enjoy each other's company, usually over lunch. We are in no way hostile to each other as we had ended that part of our karmic lesson.

All karma is administered by us, and only we can be held responsible for our life experience.

- No one can escape their karma.
- All karma is acted out in the earthly plane; we cannot undo karma in Heaven.
- All karma has to be undone before we can ascend to a higher realm.

Chapter Twenty-Five
Anger

EVERYONE HAS BEEN angry at one time or another, and there are some people who seem to be angry all the time. Anger was created after separation. It is an expression of our fear that God would punish us for separating from Him. We all know what makes us angry, and some of our anger has been brought forward from other lifetimes. Sometimes we can get angry very quickly, either at ourselves or someone else, and we are sometimes surprised when anger raises its ugly head. It is a reaction, not a planned event.

When we feel angry, it is usually over something minor that we perceive as irritating and has set us off, resulting in someone getting an earful when we express our feelings. Being angry at ourselves or someone else is an ego attack against ourselves either way. You are hurting yourself because your ego is controlling your actions. If we cannot control our anger, it can lead to abuse and physical attack against another, which is not acceptable and creates bad karma.

While under Holy Spirit's tutelage, all misperceptions and beliefs that contain anger will be purified and the anger released as our minds are healed.

- Anger is an attack by your ego against yourself or someone else.
- Anger causes guilt, fear, and unhappiness.

Bob's Commentary

We see cases of extreme anger every day on television, at the movies, in video games, and in the newspapers, and these, in turn, foster anger, particularly in our young people. When we observe anger displayed in the media or in a show, we are being misguided into thinking that it is an appropriate and acceptable way to behave. Without knowing better, we continue to create more negative karma in future lives. We become trapped in the ego-motivated cycle of cause and effect. This does not allow us to recognize that we are responsible for our thoughts and actions. We have free will to decide on a peaceful solution to an angry dispute.

Chapter Twenty-Six
Fear versus Love

PLANET EARTH IS a fear-based reality. Those of us who incarnate on this planet do so to experience fear, pain, and suffering, and to overcome those feelings. There are only two emotions on the earthly plane: one is true and the other we have made and is an illusion. We see or perceive either through love or fear. We judge those around us based on how we originally perceived them. Our perceptions of others are based on karma and our current life experiences.

With the exception of love, which is real, all other emotions are fear-based, and we have applied numerous labels to them, such as anger, guilt, envy, greed, betrayal, revenge, disgust, shame, embarrassment, and paranoia.

If we are fearful, we believe in judging others, which creates guilt and unhappiness within.

We are fearful of many things, some of which have been brought forward in our cellular memory from other lifetimes. Fear at one time or another has prevented us from doing something or going somewhere. The most common fear we have is that of other people because the ego is fearful of everyone.

The basis for all fear comes from our subconscious belief that we are separate from God and are on our own in this frightening place. There is this great negativity and fear of the people on this planet. There are so many people holding the fear vibration that they are polluting the planet with their negativity.

Fear is the opposite of love. The more fearful we are, the less likely we are to love ourselves than someone who is less fearful. If we don't love ourselves, we cannot love someone else and maintain a loving relationship.

When we accept Atonement, Holy Spirit

dispels our fears as He heals our negative thoughts. As our fears are dispelled, more love and happiness are allowed into our awareness to replace the fear.

- Fear can control and manipulate.
- Fear is inspired by the ego.
- Fear is the opposite of love.

Chapter Twenty-Seven
Pain, Pleasure, and Sickness

PAIN, PLEASURE, AND sickness are all illusions created by our egos and are not real, although they feel very real. They are all components of our dream states. Pain may appear to be the result of having injured ourselves; for example, we may have fallen and banged our knee or sprained an ankle. We feel physical pain as well as emotional upset. Pain can come in the form of an annoying ache or pain anywhere in our bodies.

No matter what the nature of our pain is, it is a reminder of an unhappy event and does not seem to be in any hurry to go away. Pain can also appear suddenly for no apparent reason. In many cases, it is pain brought forward from a former lifetime in our cellular memory. It is activated by a thought or event. Many people blame God or someone else for all their problems. No one other than ourselves is responsible for our problems. Pain is a form of punishment created by the ego and is another form of attack against us. It reminds us of our misperceived thoughts and beliefs.

Pain and pleasure were created by our egos for the same purpose to demonstrate that the body is real and can be hurt, and to draw our attention away from thinking of God. Pain, while created by the ego, is connected to our negative thoughts and feelings associated with ourselves and others.

Sickness, like pain and pleasure, is a condition of the mind and not of the body. The ego created sick-ness, which is a form of guilt as a defense against truth. Its purpose is to conceal and distort reality and pre-occupy our thoughts and time so we cannot hear God. The ego uses sickness as an attack against the body to convince us of our vulnerability. It is a symptom of our desire to be special. Contrary to popular belief, the body cannot become ill. All illness is created in the mind. We all have this imagined belief that we will eventually get sick and die. This is an ego concept to tell us we are fragile and our weaknesses will be our end. Holy Spirit teaches us that we are finite only while in a body. The soul is infinite and eternal, and is not the body.

Holy Spirit sees health as the natural state of everything. Perfect health is the result when we cease to use our bodies and minds in an unloving manner. By choosing Atonement and allowing Holy Spirit to heal our minds of all negative thoughts through forgiveness, perfect health can be attained.

- Sickness was not created by God.
- You eventually become sick when you place little value on yourself.
- All sickness came about from our perceived separation from God.
- Sickness is anger taken out against the body so it will suffer pain and eventually die.

Since I chose Atonement, I have had numerous improvements in my health, and every now and then I notice a further improvement in my overall well-being. I am healthier today than I was twenty years ago. I am not judging anyone who is sick. This isn't the reason for this information. There are many reasons why we write a life script incorporating illness. The life lessons need to be respected. We can, however, change the intensity of illness and choose to defeat it once we have learned the lesson. When the lesson no longer serves us, we can let it go. It is, after all, our choice. Our free will guided by Holy Spirit is a wonderful option.

Chapter Twenty-Eight
Victims

IN TODAY'S SOCIETY, many people are mired in the role of being a victim and cannot see themselves as being anything else. Everyone has been a victim at one time or another in their lifetime. Many have been playing the victim role for many lifetimes and are unable to break out of what has now become a traditional role for them.

I am going to focus on those who perceive themselves as victims. Those with the victim mentality are forever complaining about how their partners, families, friends, strangers, religions, and governments take advantage of them. What you don't realize is that when you believe you are a victim, you attract those to you who like victimizing people like you. If you are a victim, you need to realize that you, and no one else, have made yourself a victim. It is your negative mindset, and only you are responsible for it. If you are a victim and are unhappy with your life, you can change to a happy and loving life simply by eliminating all negative perceptions through the Atonement process. You have the free will to accept change in your life story through Atonement. It is choice, and only your choice, to do so.

Victims are very unhappy people who like telling their victim stories to whoever will listen, which, in turn, reinforces their victim role and their belief in who they are. They feel special in their role and perceive the attention they gain from it as good attention. They don't realize it keeps their victim cycle going.

- A victim is a sad example of how the ego can attack you.
- Victims blame everyone else for their problems, not realizing it is they who created their victim role.
- People who like to rescue victims are usually victims themselves and see the trait in others.

156

- Holy Spirit does not recognize anyone as being a victim and is waiting for them to accept Atonement to heal their minds.

Bob's Commentary

We have met many people who consider themselves victims and who are not ready for Atonement. Someday they will be ready; however, in the meantime they will have further unhappy lifetimes, not realizing they have created their victim mindset.

Deborah's Commentary

There can be pride in victimhood. I was at a workshop in which another attendee stated that he was a martyr, and that was his way to one-up the person next to him who was playing the victim role. He was proud of his sad state and didn't accept that he had any choice in the matter or that he could heal himself. He simply continued this role because he enjoyed the attention he received from the women who wanted to rescue him. I thought it was a unique pick-up line, but totally defeating because negative karma was being created at an alarming rate.

Chapter Twenty-Nine
Peace of Heaven

THE BIBLE TELLS us the Peace of God passeth all
understanding. We all enjoyed this Peace of Heaven
before our perceived separation from God. Very few
have claimed to have felt this peace on earth, and
those who have cannot fully experience it in this
physical form. When you work with the Holy Spirit,
you receive inner peace. Initially, inner peace seems
to sneak into your awareness, and you recognize it
because it is like nothing you have ever experienced
before on earth. When your peace increases, you
notice a constant calmness that does not change,
regardless of the dramas or upsets you may be faced
with in your day-to-day life. This peace and
calmness is as close as possible to experiencing
Heaven on earth.

- There is no substitute for peace.
- Peace is the ultimate drug to keep you happy, and it is free.
- To have peace, you must teach it to learn it.
- God wills us to be in Heaven, and nothing can keep us from it.

Bob's Commentary

I have enjoyed peace and its calmness for some time now, and I savor it. Peace is a constant state of mind that does not allow any silly ego chatter or upset to enter. Nothing seems to bother or upset me, no matter how disturbing it may be to others. Peace of mind provides me with clarity of thought and a state of well-being. I am very aware of my peace, which provides me with increasing comfort and an awareness of who I truly am.

Chapter Thirty
Remembering God

GOD IS THE creator of all souls, and every living creature on this planet and elsewhere has a soul. Since our perceived separation from God, over eons we created blockages to prevent our memory of Him and our creation story. No one can remember God, and there are many who believe God does not exist. Most of us have no conscious thoughts or memories of God in our lives.

We created the ego to replace God, and it has been very effective in helping us to forget that God created us, and it keeps us from remembering who we truly are. God has willed us to awaken from our dream state and return to Him, and there is nothing more powerful than His will. It is because of God's love for us, and our free will, that He has not intervened in our free will or our temptation to deny Him.

Remembering who and what we are will come to us only after Holy Spirit has purified our minds of all the ego's negative thoughts and beliefs. After you have accepted Atonement, you will receive Holy Spirit's miracle healings. When you receive a few healings that would not have happened had you not accepted Atonement, you will realize that Holy Spirit resides in your mind, and that what the Course is teaching is true. The memory of God comes to the quiet mind as it cannot come to a mind that is filled with conflict and ego chatter.

- Faith in God is always justified, for God is kind and loving.
- The wisest thing anyone can do is to seek God.
- By improving our goodness, we can acquire peace and well-being.
- God has given us the means to undo what we have made.
- The Course tells us God guarantees that no one can fail Atonement.

162

Deborah and I had an interesting experience a few years ago that we wish to share with you. Several friends on different occasions had suggested we go to the Bancroft Annual Gemboree. The event draws people from all over North America to view and purchase crystals from numerous vendors, who themselves come from faraway places. We decided to attend the event and left at 7 a.m. on a very bright, sunny Friday morning. It took us a few minutes to reach the highway, and when we turned on to it, we found the bright sunlight was in our faces. We pulled down our visors, and it was a few seconds later that I noticed what appeared to be a gold reflection off the car's hood. I thought the reflection was unusual and decided to raise my visor for a better view. What I saw was breathtaking. It was a two-inch-wide golden arc that traveled all the way to the sun. I then noticed a small golden branch from the arc stretched to the hood on Deborah's side of the car. This golden arc stayed with us all the way to Bancroft—for approximately three hours. It did not matter whether we were shaded at times from the sun, the arc remained. When we decided to return home later that afternoon, the golden arc remained with us until we arrived home. Later, we asked We Are One about the golden arc, and we were told that this was Holy Spirit telling us He was with us and we were safely protected in his love.

When you work with spirit, many things that seem unusual to others can occur. We had decided to paint the inside of our home. The evening before the morning I was going to start to paint, I decided to remove the pictures from the front hallway. The first picture I removed was a framed print of a great horned owl that I had acquired ten years earlier. When I sat the picture down against the wall, I noticed what appeared to be a brownish-red stain on the wall where the picture had hung. This stain was two to three inches high and about twenty inches wide—the width of the picture. On closer examination, I found the stain was raised and slightly damp. I was perplexed and could not understand where this stain could have possibly come from. Finally, I picked up the picture and turned it around and found the backing on the bottom of the picture was wet to the touch. This was a real mystery to Deborah and me. We decided to ask We Are One. They told us the picture was bleeding, and it was blood that was congealed on the wall. We were told that Holy Spirit was sending us a message, which was that we needed to become closer to nature. We needed to offer a blessing for the animal spirits each time we held a group at our home, which we did. When you bring Holy Spirit into your life, many unusual things can occur. Observe Holy Spirit's signs, as they are on the map of understanding on your chosen path.

Chapter Thirty-One
Defenses against God

SINCE SEPARATION, OUR ego consciousness has created numerous forms of defense to prevent us from remembering God and His love for us. We have also forgotten that we are divine spiritual beings and not physical beings with egos.

I have touched on some of these defenses throughout the book and will now highlight a few of them. Virtually every single thing we do has been designed to support our subconscious belief in our separation from God and one another, as well as the fact that we no longer reside in Heaven. The initial defense we created was the ego to replace God.

We have created numerous activities to distract ourselves from thinking about God and our own destiny. These activities include arts, crafts, sports, gardening, TV, video games, and work. Although the ego is not real and is part of our dreams, we have given it power and at times are afraid of its frightening thoughts. When we created the ego, it turned against us, and every problem people have had is due to their egos. You now know more about your ego than before, and you cannot undo your ego without the assistance of Holy Spirit. To try doing it without the Holy Spirit's assistance, you will be using your ego to undo itself, and this will not work. This only temporarily buries it. You can never be completely free from your ego because it is responsible for body functions. You can, however, minimize its power in your life choices by allowing Holy Spirit to assist you in making daily decisions that avoid creating further fear, anger, guilt, and unhappiness. As long as your mind chooses to hold an earthly image, it needs an ego. We believe what the ego tells us because we created it, and because we cannot remember God. Virtually everything the ego tells us is untrue, which is why Holy Spirit is required to purify our ego thought systems.

We have all heard stories where someone has done inhumane things to another and claimed God told him to do it. God, who is loving and kind, would not tell anyone to harm another person. We are all God's children and equal in God's love. What the person heard was his ego speaking to him. Those who do harm to others are unable to discern between right and wrong and are under the control of their egos, which they have allowed to control them. People who do unspeakable things are considered insane by Heaven's standards. Many who are under the ego's control have far more personal problems than those who have some control over their egos. The more control our egos have, the greater the chances our lives are living hell. Hell is not a place, but a state of mind. The Course says that when you are insane, you don't realize it. Our prisons are full of the insane, who have allowed their egos to take control.

The ego has convinced us our bodies are real and created pain, sickness, depression, and death to prove the body is real. The ego has made death attractive when we become sick and miserable. The ego doesn't tell us we will simply create a new body and begin the cycle of guilt, fear, anger, unhappiness, sickness, and death all over again. Holy Spirit tells us death is part of the illusion like all the other illusions the ego has created.

Our decision to create and follow a new consciousness eons ago no longer serves humanity. God has willed us to return to Him and gave us Atonement to speed up the process. If you want to continue living in this insane world, that is your choice. The time is now that we all need to reconnect to our God Source and move on to higher spiritual realms in eternity, where the focus is on love, peace, happiness, and oneness. As the earth consciousness evolves, the old ego ways will become less agreeable. Those of you who are reading this information and wish to be part of the healing solution will no longer support the problems of earth and modern society.

Chapter Thirty-Two
Ascension and the New Earth

AT THIS TIME on the planet, there is a divine plan unfolding that will affect the consciousness of every single person on the planet and open every heart to a higher level of unconditional love. This divine plan was referred to in the Bible as the *shift* and was prophesized thousands of years ago. This is a shift in mankind's consciousness to a higher level of vibration.

Every person, at their soul level, chose to be here on the planet at this time to experience the conscious shift and heart opening. This shift is known as *Ascension*. A new fourth-dimensional earth has been created for those who wish to ascend. For some time now, there have been energies directed toward the planet to gradually increase the level of consciousness for everyone. Over the next few years, you will have to decide whether you wish to stay on three-dimensional earth or ascend to the new fourth-dimensional earth. Everyone who ascends must have healed themselves of all negativity and opened their heart centers for unconditional love. The new earth will be based on unconditional love, rather than on fear, on this planet. On the new earth, there will be no disease or illness. There will be no need for shopping malls, for if you need something, you will be able to instantly create it. There will be no need for vehicles, for if you wish to visit someone, you will instantly be there. There will be many more positive changes. The new earth will be the first level of Heaven.

The Second Coming referred to in the Bible is not one Messiah, but rather 144,000 Christed beings who have been strategically placed around the planet. When this group completes what is called a *soul-merge*, they will create a single body of light around the planet. This energy will change everyone's fear-based three-dimensional love to fourth-dimensional unconditional love, provided you permit it. This energy will create the first stage of soul-merging for everyone. The second stage involves the healing of all emotional traumas in your life. The third stage is the connecting of your soul with your heart. All these stages will be profound experiences, preparing you for ascension. There will be many on the planet who will resist opening their hearts to unconditional love, which will prevent them from ascending to the new earth. This is certainly a great time to be on this planet for those who wish to move on to the next level of their spiritual journey.

Epilogue

WE HAVE SPOKEN about many hidden truths that
have been kept from us for a very long time, and
there are many more. We all have to learn about
truth at one time or another, and because it conflicts
with our current belief system, we require Holy
Spirit to purify our minds and teach us in a gentle
manner. There are many layers to our consciousness,
all of which have to be healed in order to merge our
ego consciousness with our higher selves, our true
selves.

No one has to change or do anything unless
they choose to do so. If you are fearful, unhappy, or
plain miserable, you probably have been for many
lifetimes and will continue in your future lifetimes
unless you choose Atonement. God created
everyone as a divine loving and peaceful being.
Why would you choose to remain unhappy when
you have a better option that is guaranteed by God?

You have to ask yourself, "What is it that I am getting from being unhappy?" Until you choose Atonement and Heaven, you will continue to live in the hell and misery your ego created.

To have faith is to heal. Faith is the opposite of fear and brings you peace and allows truth to enter your consciousness. Faith is having an inner belief that there is a higher spiritual source that we can look to and pray to. The *Course in Miracles* text was created to assist us in our spiritual evolution. It is a great tool, and is specifically designed as an aid to mind-healing. It has been of tremendous help to both Deborah and me on our journeys home.

The shift in consciousness underway on the planet will impact every single person. How this shift will affect each one of us depends on how much we allow it. If you are fearful of awakening to your higher-self mind and unconditional love, you may limit yourself and may not complete your soul-merge at this time, which is required to ascend to the new fourth-dimensional earth.

176

As the Course, which is required, tells us, only the time it takes to read and study it is voluntary on our journey home.

Blessings Be with You

Glossary

Ascended Masters: Spiritually advanced beings who have gone through a series of initiations/ spiritual transformations. They live in the fifth and higher dimensions.

Akashic records: A library of the human experience of every person since the beginning of separation. The records are constantly updated. A person can access his or her records by using hypnosis.

Council of 144,000 Ascended Masters: A council of ascended masters who administer the middle and lower heavens. They also hold the more senior positions in earth's spiritual government.

Free will: The ability that humans have to make their own choices by using their higher-self minds or their lower-self minds and putting their choices into action.

Reincarnation: A concept that we create a new body after a physical or biological death.

About the Authors

Robert (Bob) Hannaford's spiritual path began about twenty years ago when he was guided to a book about reincarnation. This and many subsequent books awakened him to the possibilities of a new world and the understanding that we are all part of a divine family. As Bob's self-awareness and knowledge grew, he was guided to living healers and prophets and discovered that he was a Lightworker and that he could help others. He soon discovered *A Course in Miracles* and studied to become a teacher of the Course. *Today's Divine Family* was born of his desire to teach others and help awaken them to the divine plan and their part in it.

Deborah Hannaford, an ordained ministerial counselor, is an active student of *A Course in Miracles* and hosts a group with her husband Bob. Deborah has always been sensitive to energies and strong emotions, and from a young age has been fascinated with concepts of ESP, telepathy, and psychic phenomena, which led her on a journey that has encompassed many healing modalities and spiritual teachings. In 2001, We Are One presented themselves to Deborah and Bob, and Deborah became a channeler of their messages and healing. We Are One are a group consciousness of spiritual beings and angels from the ninth hierarchy who are God's Advisory Council.

Notes

Notes

Notes

Notes

Notes

Notes